THE ULTIMATE BULGARIAN PHRASE BOOK

1001 BULGARIAN PHRASES FOR BEGINNERS AND BEYOND!

BY ADRIAN GEE

ISBN: 979-8-872981-89-3

Author's Note

Welcome to "The Ultimate Bulgarian Phrase Book"! It's with great joy and enthusiasm that I invite you to embark on a captivating journey into the soul of Bulgarian – a language steeped in a rich tapestry of history and imbued with the warmth of Slavic charm. Whether your fascination lies in the rugged beauty of the Balkan Mountains, the enchanting streets of Sofia, or the vibrant cultural traditions that pulse through Bulgaria, this book is meticulously crafted to ensure your path to learning Bulgarian is as delightful and fulfilling as possible.

As a passionate linguist and an ardent proponent of cultural immersion, I recognize the intricate art of mastering a new language. This book emerges from that recognition, aiming to be an invaluable guide on your journey towards Bulgarian proficiency.

Connect with Me: The adventure of learning a language extends beyond mastering words and grammar; it's an exhilarating expedition into connecting with people and understanding the spirit of a unique culture. I warmly invite you to join me and fellow language enthusiasts on Instagram: @adriangruszka, where we share knowledge, experiences, and celebrate our linguistic journeys.

Sharing is Caring: If this book becomes a pivotal tool in your language learning journey, I would be deeply honored by your recommendation to others who share a passion for the diverse linguistic heritage of our world. If you wish to share your experiences or celebrate your successes in Bulgarian on Instagram, please tag me – I am excited to cheer on your achievements!

Embarking on the Bulgarian language journey is like exploring a land rich with historical depth, enduring traditions, and a strong sense of community. Embrace the challenges, cherish your progress, and relish every moment of your Bulgarian adventure.

Наслука! (Good luck!)

- Adrian Gee

CONTENTS

INTRODUCTION

Добре дошли! (Welcome!)

Whether you're envisioning a stroll through the quaint streets of Plovdiv, planning an adventure in the Rila Mountains, eager to connect with Bulgarian speakers, or simply drawn to the Bulgarian language out of sheer fascination, this phrase book is crafted to be your trusty companion.

Embarking on the Bulgarian language journey invites you into a world rich in history, vibrant folklore, and a profound appreciation for the arts and nature. Bulgarian, with its melodious tones and rhythmic nuances, offers a unique window into the soul of the Balkans.

Защо Български? (Why Bulgarian?)

With over 8 million native speakers, Bulgarian is not just the language of the mystic Balkan Mountains and the serene Black Sea coast but also a key to understanding the region's rich history and cultural diversity. As an official language of the European Union and spoken across several countries, it is a vital tool for explorers, historians, business professionals, and everyone enchanted by its distinctive charm.

Произношение (Pronunciation)

Before diving into the extensive collection of phrases and expressions, it's crucial to acquaint yourself with the essence of the Bulgarian language. Each language dances to its rhythm, and Bulgarian is no exception, with its harmonic balance of softness and resonance. Initially, its pronunciation might appear challenging, but with consistent practice, the clear vowel sounds and the rhythmic cadence of Bulgarian can enrich your language skills.

Bulgarian pronunciation is characterized by its stress patterns and distinct consonant sounds. The language's rhythmic flow, the resonance of its vowels, and the specific stress on syllables create a melody that is both intriguing and inviting. Mastering pronunciation not only aids in clear communication but also helps you connect more deeply with the essence of Bulgarian culture and its people.

Българската Азбука (The Bulgarian Alphabet)

The Bulgarian alphabet is a Cyrillic script and consists of 30 letters. Some letters might look familiar to those used in Latin scripts, but many have unique sounds that might be unfamiliar to English speakers.

Гласни (Vowels)

А (а): Like the "a" in "father."
Е (е): Similar to the "e" in "bed."
И (и): Like the "ee" in "see."
О (о): Like the "o" in "bore."
У (у): Similar to the "oo" in "food."
Ъ (ъ): A hard sound, somewhat like the "a" in "about."
Ь (ь): Indicates a softening of the preceding consonant, not a vowel on its own.
Ю (ю): Like the "u" in "use."
Я (я): Similar to the "ya" in "yard."

Съгласни (Consonants).

Б (б): Like the "b" in "bat."
В (в): Like the "v" in "van."
Г (г): Like the "g" in "go."
Д (д): Similar to the "d" in "dog."
Ж (ж): Similar to the "s" in "pleasure."
З (з): Like the "z" in "zoo."

Й (й): Similar to the "y" in "boy."
К (к): Like the "k" in "kite."
Л (л): Like the "l" in "love."
М (м): Like the "m" in "mother."
Н (н): Like the "n" in "nice."
П (п): Like the "p" in "pen."
Р (р): A rolling "r," pronounced at the front of the mouth.
С (с): Like the "s" in "see."
Т (т): Like the "t" in "top."
Ф (ф): Like the "f" in "far."
Х (х): Similar to the "h" in "hello" or the "ch" in Scottish "loch."
Ц (ц): Like the "ts" in "cats."
Ч (ч): Like the "ch" in "chop."
Ш (ш): Like the "sh" in "shop."
Щ (щ): Similar to "sht" in "wishful."

It's important to note that the Cyrillic script used in Bulgarian is distinct from other alphabets and requires dedicated practice to master its unique characters and sounds.

Bulgarian Intonation and Stress Patterns

Bulgarian intonation possesses a rhythmic and melodic quality, which is characteristic of Slavic languages. Typically, stress in Bulgarian words falls on the penultimate (second-to-last) syllable, which is a distinguishing feature and important to grasp for correct pronunciation.

Common Pronunciation Challenges

Сложни Гласни Комбинации (Complex Vowel Combinations)

Bulgarian has a set of vowel sounds that may be new to English speakers. Mastering these is essential. Additionally, the Bulgarian language features consonant clusters that can be challenging but are integral to mastering the language's unique character.

Tips for Practicing Pronunciation

1. **Слушайте Внимателно (Listen Carefully):** Listening to Bulgarian music, podcasts, and watching Bulgarian movies is an excellent way to familiarize yourself with the language's rhythm and melody.

2. **Повтаряйте След Носител на Езика (Repeat After a Native Speaker):** Engaging with native Bulgarian speakers, in person or through language exchange platforms, is invaluable for refining your pronunciation.

3. **Използвайте Огледало (Use a Mirror):** Watching your own mouth movements can help ensure that your articulation of Bulgarian sounds is precise.

4. **Упражнявайте се Редовно (Practice Regularly):** Consistent practice, even if it's just for a few minutes each day, is key to improving your skills.

5. **Не се Страхувайте от Грешки (Don't Fear Mistakes):** Embrace errors as they are a natural part of the learning journey and lead to better understanding and proficiency.

Clear pronunciation is fundamental to navigating the intricate soundscape of Bulgarian. Commit to mastering its distinct sounds, from the resonant vowels to the vibrant consonant clusters, and observe as the language unfolds like the rich Bulgarian folklore. Each phonetic nuance captures the essence of Bulgaria's storied history and culture.

What You'll Find Inside

- **Важни Фрази (Essential Phrases):** Thoughtfully curated sentences and expressions for various situations you may encounter in Bulgarian-speaking environments.

- **Интерактивни Упражнения (Interactive Exercises):** Engaging exercises designed to test and improve your language skills and encourage active use of Bulgarian.

- **Културни Прозрения (Cultural Insights):** Delve into the rich tapestry of Bulgarian-speaking regions, from their social norms to their historical sites.

- **Допълнителни Ресурси (Additional Resources):** A compilation of further materials and advice for enhancing your Bulgarian language proficiency, including websites, book recommendations, and travel tips.

How to Use This Phrase Book

This book has been carefully crafted to support beginners embarking on their initial exploration of Bulgarian, as well as intermediate learners seeking to deepen their linguistic skills. Start your journey with essential phrases suitable for a variety of situations, from basic greetings to navigating the nuances of Bulgarian social customs. As you gain confidence, progress to more complex language structures and idiomatic expressions that will bring you closer to the fluency of a native speaker.

Within these pages, you'll find cultural insights that connect you more deeply with Bulgaria's rich history and vibrant present. Interactive exercises are strategically interspersed to reinforce your learning and help you seamlessly incorporate new words and grammar into your conversations.

Learning a language is an adventure that transcends memorization—it's an engaging, continuous pursuit of connection. Dive into Bulgarian dialogues, explore the country's illustrious literary offerings, and embrace the customs that weave the fabric of this distinctive culture.

Each individual's journey to language mastery is unique, characterized by its own rhythm and milestones. Nurture your skills with patience, passion, and a sense of exploration. With dedicated practice, your proficiency and confidence in Bulgarian will not just improve; they will flourish.

Готови ли сте да започнете? (Ready to start?)

Embark on an enlightening journey into the heart of the Bulgarian language and culture. Unravel its linguistic intricacies and immerse yourself in the cultural richness that Bulgaria offers. This journey promises to be as rewarding as it is transformative, expanding your horizons and enriching your global understanding.

GREETINGS & INTRODUCTIONS

- BASIC GREETINGS -
- INTRODUCING YOURSELF AND OTHERS -
- EXPRESSING POLITENESS AND FORMALITY -

Basic Greetings

1. Hi!
   Здрасти!
   (Zdrah-stee!)

2. Hello!
   Здравей!
   (Zdrah-vey!)

   > **Idiomatic Expression:** "Като на майната си." -
   > Meaning: "At ease, very comfortable."
   > (Literal Translation: "Like at one's mother's place.")

3. Good morning!
   Добро утро!
   (Doh-broh oo-troh!)

   > **Cultural Insight:** On March 1st, Bulgarians celebrate
   > Baba Marta Day by exchanging red and white
   > adornments called 'martenitsi', symbolizing health and
   > happiness.

4. Good afternoon!
   Добър ден!
   (Doh-bur dehn!)

5. Good evening!
   Добър вечер!
   (Doh-bur veh-cher!)

6. How are you?
   Как си?
   (Kahk see?)

> **Cultural Insight:** Celebrating name days is as important as birthdays in Bulgaria. It's a tradition where people named after a saint celebrate on that saint's feast day.

7. Everything good?
   Всичко добре?
   (Vseech-koh doh-breh?)

8. How is it going?
   Как върви?
   (Kahk vur-vee?)

9. How is everything?
   Как е всичко?
   (Kahk eh vseech-koh?)

10. I'm good, thank you.
    Добре съм, благодаря.
    (Doh-breh sum, blah-goh-da-ryah.)

11. And you?
    А ти?
    (Ah tee?)

12. Let me introduce...
    Нека ви представя...
    (Neh-kah vee prehd-stahv-yah...)

13. This is...
    Това е...
    (Toh-vah eh...)

14. Nice to meet you!
Приятно ми е да се запознаем!
(Pree-yat-noh mee eh dah seh zah-poz-nah-em!)

15. Delighted!
Много съм радостен/радостна!
(Mnoh-goh sum rah-dohs-ten/rah-dohs-tah!)

16. How have you been?
Как сте? (formal) / Как си? (informal)
(Kahk steh?) / (Kahk see?)

Politeness and Formality

17. Excuse me.
Извинете.
(Eez-vee-neh-teh.)

18. Please.
Моля.
(Moh-lyah.)

19. Thank you.
Благодаря.
(Blah-goh-dah-ryah.)

> **Fun Fact:** Bulgaria is the oldest country in Europe that hasn't changed its name since it was first established in 681 AD.

20. Thank you very much!
Много благодаря!
(Mnoh-goh blah-goh-dah-ryah!)

21. I'm sorry.
    Съжалявам.
    (Suh-zha-lyah-vahm.)

22. I apologize.
    Извинявам се.
    (Eez-veen-yah-vahm seh.)

23. Sir
    Господин
    (Gohs-poh-deen)

24. Madam
    Госпожа
    (Gohs-poh-zhah)

25. Miss
    Госпожица
    (Gohs-poh-zhee-tsah)

26. Your name, please?
    Как се казвате?
    (Kahk seh kahz-vah-teh?)

27. Can I help you with anything?
    Мога ли да Ви помогна с нещо?
    (Moh-gah lee dah vee poh-mohg-nah s neh-shtoh?)

28. I am thankful for your help.
    Благодаря за помощта Ви.
    (Blah-goh-dah-ryah zah poh-mohsht-tah vee.)

29. The pleasure is mine.
    Удоволствието е мое.
    (Oo-doh-vohl-stvee-eh-toh eh moh-eh.)

30. Thank you for your hospitality.
Благодаря за гостоприемството.
(Blah-goh-dah-ryah zah gohs-toh-pree-em-stvoh-toh.)

31. It's nice to see you again.
Радвам се да те видя отново.
(Rahd-vahm seh dah teh vee-dyah ot-noh-voh.)

Greetings for Different Times of Day

32. Good morning, my friend!
Добро утро, приятелю!
(Doh-broh oo-troh, pree-ya-teh-lyoo!)

33. Good afternoon, colleague!
Добър ден, колега!
(Doh-bur dehn, koh-leh-gah!)

34. Good evening neighbor!
Добър вечер, съседе!
(Doh-bur veh-cher, suh-seh-deh!)

35. Have a good night!
Лека нощ!
(Leh-kah noh-sht!)

36. Sleep well!
Спи добре!
(Spee doh-breh!)

Special Occasions

37. Happy birthday!
Честит рожден ден!
(Cheh-stit rohzh-den dehn!)

> **Language Learning Tip:** Listen to Bulgarian Music - It helps with learning pronunciation and rhythm.

38. Merry Christmas!
Весела Коледа!
(Veh-seh-lah Koh-leh-dah!)

39. Happy Easter!
Весел Великден!
(Veh-sehl Veh-lee-kden!)

> **Travel Story:** In the heart of Sofia, at the bustling Vitosha Boulevard, a street artist painted the vibrant city life, whispering, "Всяко нещо си има красота" (Every thing has its beauty), reminding me of the charm in everyday scenes.

40. Happy holidays!
Весели празници!
(Veh-seh-lee prahz-nee-tsee!)

41. Happy New Year!
Честита Нова Година!
(Cheh-stee-tah No-vah Goh-dee-nah!)

> **Idiomatic Expression:** "На кучето му е пръснало." - Meaning: "It doesn't matter at all."
> (Literal Translation: "The dog has burst.")

Meeting Someone for the First Time

42. Pleasure to meet you.
    Приятно ми е да се запознаем.
    (Pree-yat-noh mee eh dah seh zah-poz-nah-em.)

> **Language Learning Tip:** Watch Bulgarian Films - With subtitles, to understand context and usage.

43. I am [Your Name].
    Казвам се [Your Name].
    (Kahz-vahm seh [Your Name].)

44. Where are you from?
    Откъде сте? (formal) / Откъде си? (informal)
    (Oht-kuh-deh steh?) / (Oht-kuh-deh see?)

> **Language Learning Tip:** Use Flashcards - They're great for memorizing vocabulary.

45. I'm on vacation.
    На почивка съм.
    (Nah poh-cheev-kah sum.)

46. What is your profession?
    Каква е вашата професия?
    (Kahk-vah eh vah-shah-tah proh-feh-see-yah?)

47. How long will you stay here?
    Колко време ще останете тук?
    (Kohl-koh vreh-meh shteh ohs-tah-neh-teh took?)

Responding to Greetings

48. Hello, how have you been?
    Здравей, как си?
    (Zdrah-vey, kahk see?)

> **Cultural Insight:** Traditional Bulgarian folk music, known for its unique rhythms and harmonies, is a significant part of cultural identity, accompanied by dances like the Horo.

49. I've been very busy lately.
    Наскоро бях много зает.
    (Nah-sko-roh byah mnoh-goh zah-et.)

50. I've had ups and downs.
    Имах своите възходи и падения.
    (Ee-mahkh svoy-teh vuz-hoh-dee ee pah-deh-nee-yah.)

> **Idiomatic Expression:** "Не му пука от високо." -
> Meaning: "He/she doesn't care at all."
> Literal Translation: "He/she doesn't care from high above."

51. Thanks for asking.
    Благодаря, че попитахте.
    (Blah-goh-dah-ryah, cheh poh-pee-tahh-teh.)

52. I feel great.
Чувствам се страхотно.
(Chuuv-stvam seh strah-hot-noh.)

53. Life has been good.
Животът е бил добър.
(Zhi-voh-tuht eh beel doh-bur.)

54. I can't complain.
Не мога да се оплача.
(Neh moh-gah dah seh oh-plah-chah.)

55. And you, how are you?
А ти, как си?
(Ah tee, kahk see?)

> **Language Learning Tip:** Speak from Day One - Don't be afraid to start speaking right away.

56. I've had some challenges.
Имах някои предизвикателства.
(Ee-mahkh nyah-koy preh-deez-vee-kah-tel-stvah.)

57. Life is a journey.
Животът е пътешествие.
(Zhi-voh-tuht eh puh-teh-shehs-tvee-eh.)

58. Thank God, I'm fine.
Слава Богу, добре съм.
(Slah-vah Boh-goo, doh-breh sum.)

Informal Greetings

59. What's up?
    Какво ново?
    (Kahk-voh noh-voh?)

60. All good?
    Всичко наред ли е?
    (Vseech-koh nah-red lee eh?)

61. Hi, everything okay?
    Здрасти, всичко наред ли е?
    (Zdrah-stee, vseech-koh nah-red lee eh?)

62. I'm good, and you?
    Добре съм, а ти?
    (Doh-breh sum, ah tee?)

63. How's life?
    Как е животът?
    (Kahk eh zhi-voh-tuht?)

64. Cool!
    Страхотно!
    (Strah-hot-noh!)

Saying Goodbye

65. Goodbye!
    Довиждане!
    (Doh-veezh-dah-neh!)

66. See you later!
   Ще се видим по-късно!
   (Shteh seh vee-deem poh-kuhs-noh!)

> **Language Learning Tip:** Practice Daily - Consistency is key in language learning.

67. Bye!
   Чао!
   (Chow!)

68. Have a good day.
   Приятен ден.
   (Pree-yah-ten dehn.)

> **Language Learning Tip:** Learn Cyrillic Script Early - Familiarize yourself with the Bulgarian alphabet.

69. Have a good weekend.
   Приятен уикенд.
   (Pree-yah-ten oo-ee-kend.)

70. Take care.
   Пази се.
   (Pah-zee seh.)

71. Bye, see you later.
   Чао, ще се видим по-късно.
   (Chow, shteh seh vee-deem poh-kuhs-noh.)

72. I need to go now.
   Трябва да тръгвам сега.
   (Tree-ab-vah dah truhg-vahm seh-gah.)

73. Take care my friend!
Пази се, приятелю!
(Pah-zee seh, pree-yah-teh-lyoo!)

Parting Words

74. Hope to see you soon.
Надявам се да се видим скоро.
(Nah-dyah-vahm seh dah seh vee-deem skoh-roh.)

75. Stay in touch.
Останете във връзка.
(Ohs-tah-neh-teh vuhv vruhz-kah.)

76. I'll miss you.
Ще ми липсваш.
(Shteh mee leep-svahsh.)

77. Be well.
Бъди добре.
(Buh-dee doh-breh.)

"Капка по капка – море се прави."
"Drop by drop – a sea is made."
Small efforts accumulate to create significant results.

Interactive Challenge: Greetings Quiz

1. **How do you say "good morning" in Bulgarian?**

    a) Какво правиш?
    b) Добро утро!
    c) Как си?

2. **What does the Bulgarian phrase "Приятно ми е да се запознаем" mean in English?**

    a) Excuse me!
    b) Pleased to meet you!
    c) How are you?

3. **When is it appropriate to use the phrase "Добър вечер!" in Bulgarian?**

    a) In the morning
    b) In the afternoon
    c) In the evening

4. **Which phrase is used to ask someone how they are doing in Bulgarian?**

    a) Благодаря
    b) Как си?
    c) Накъде отиваш?

5. **In Bulgaria, when can you use the greeting "Здравей!"?**

    a) Only in the morning
    b) Only in the afternoon
    c) Anytime

6. **What is the Bulgarian equivalent of "And you?"?**

   a) А ти?
   b) Благодаря
   c) Какво правиш?

7. **When expressing gratitude in Bulgarian, what do you say?**

   a) Извинете
   b) Приятно ми е да се запознаем
   c) Благодаря

8. **How do you say "Excuse me" in Bulgarian?**

   a) Извинете
   b) Добър следобед!
   c) Всичко наред ли е?

9. **Which phrase is used to inquire about someone's well-being?**

   a) Къде живееш?
   b) Как си?
   c) Благодаря

10. **In a typical Bulgarian conversation, when is it common to ask about someone's background and interests during a first-time meeting?**

   a) Never
   b) Only in formal situations
   c) Always

11. In Bulgarian, what does "Приятно ми е да се запознаем" mean?

    a) Delighted to meet you
    b) Excuse me
    c) Thank you

12. When should you use the phrase "Как си?"?

    a) When ordering food
    b) When asking for directions
    c) When inquiring about someone's well-being

13. Which phrase is used to make requests politely?

    a) Как си?
    b) Какво искаш?
    c) Моля

14. What is the equivalent of "I'm sorry" in Bulgarian?

    a) Съжалявам
    b) Как си?
    c) Всичко е наред

Correct Answers:

1. b)
2. b)
3. c)
4. b)
5. c)
6. a)
7. c)
8. a)
9. b)
10. c)
11. a)
12. c)
13. c)
14. a)

EATING & DINING

- ORDERING FOOD AND DRINKS IN A RESTAURANT -
- DIETARY PREFERENCES AND RESTRICTIONS -
- COMPLIMENTS AND COMPLAINTS ABOUT FOOD -

Basic Ordering

78. I'd like a table for two, please.
Бих искал маса за двама, моля.
(Beeh ees-kahl mah-sah zah dvah-mah, moh-lyah.)

79. What's the special of the day?
Какво е специалитетът на деня?
(Kahk-voh eh speh-tsee-ah-lee-teht-uht nah dehn-yah?)

> **Cultural Insight:** The period of Communist rule (1946-1989) significantly shaped modern Bulgarian society, and its remnants are still visible in architecture and social attitudes.

80. Can I see the menu, please?
Мога ли да видя менюто, моля?
(Moh-gah lee dah vee-dyah meh-nyoo-toh, moh-lyah?)

81. I'll have the steak, medium rare.
Ще взема стек, средно изпечен.
(Shteh vze-mah stek, srehd-noh eez-peh-chen.)

82. Can I get a glass of water?
Мога ли да получа чаша вода, моля?
(Moh-gah lee dah poh-loo-chah chah-shah voh-dah, moh-lyah?)

> **Travel Story:** On the serene shores of the Black Sea in Burgas, an old fisherman mended his net, murmuring, "В тихата вода и дяволът се дави" (In still water, even the devil drowns), reflecting on life's unexpected challenges.

83. Can you bring us some bread to start?
   Можете ли да ни донесете хляб за начало?
   (Moh-zheh-teh lee dah nee doh-ne-seh-teh khlyahb zah nah-chah-loh?)

84. Do you have a vegetarian option?
   Имате ли вегетарианска опция?
   (Ee-mah-teh lee veh-geh-tah-ree-ahn-skah op-tsya?)

> **Language Learning Tip:** Use Language Apps - Apps like Duolingo or Babbel can be helpful for beginners.

85. Is there a kids' menu available?
   Имате ли детско меню?
   (Ee-mah-teh lee deht-skoh meh-nyoo?)

86. We'd like to order appetizers to share.
   Бихме искали да поръчаме предястия за споделяне.
   (Beeh-meh ees-kah-lee dah poh-ruh-chah-meh preh-dyah-stee-ah zah spoh-deh-lyah-neh.)

87. Can we have separate checks, please?
   Можем ли да имаме отделни сметки, моля?
   (Moh-zhem lee dah ee-mah-meh oht-dehl-nee smet-kee, moh-lyah?)

88. Could you recommend a vegetarian dish?
   Можете ли да препоръчате вегетарианско ястие?
   (Moh-zheh-teh lee dah preh-poh-ruh-chah-teh veh-geh-tah-ree-ahn-skoh yah-stee-eh?)

89. I'd like to try the local cuisine.
   Бих искал да опитам местната кухня.
   (Beeh ees-kahl dah oh-pee-tahm mehst-nah-tah koo-hnyah.)

90. May I have a refill on my drink, please?

Може ли да ми напълните отново напитката, моля?

(Moh-zheh lee dah mee nah-puhl-nee-teh oht-noh-voh nah-pee-tkah-tah, moh-lyah?)

91. What's the chef's special today?

Какво е днешното специално предложение от главния готвач?

(Kahk-voh eh dnehsh-noh-toh speh-tsee-ahl-noh prehd-loh-zheh-nee-eh oht glahv-nee-yah goht-vahch?)

92. Can you make it extra spicy?

Можете ли да го направите по-лют, моля?

(Moh-zheh-teh lee dah goh nah-prah-vee-teh poh-lyoot, moh-lyah?)

93. I'll have the chef's tasting menu.

Ще взема дегустационното меню на главния готвач.

(Shteh vze-mah deh-goo-stah-tsee-on-noh-toh meh-nyoo nah glahv-nee-yah goht-vahch.)

Special Requests

94. I'm allergic to nuts. Is this dish nut-free?

Алергичен/алергична съм към ядки. Без ядки ли е това ястие?

(Ah-lehr-gee-chen/ah-lehr-gee-chnah sum kuhm yahd-kee. Behz yahd-kee lee eh toh-vah yah-stee-eh?)

95. I'm on a gluten-free diet. What can I have?

Спазвам диета без глутен. Какво мога да поръчам?

(Spahz-vahm dee-eh-tah behz gloo-ten. Kahk-voh moh-gah dah poh-ruh-chahm?)

96. Can you make it less spicy, please?
Можете ли да го направите по-малко лют, моля?
(Moh-zheh-teh lee dah goh nah-prah-vee-teh poh-mahl-koh lyoot, moh-lyah?)

> **Idiomatic Expression:** "Хванат с крачол."
> - Meaning: "Caught in the act."
> (Literal translation: "Caught by the leg.")

97. Can you recommend a local specialty?
Можете ли да препоръчате местна специалност?
(Moh-zheh-teh lee dah preh-poh-ruh-chah-teh mehst-nah speh-tsee-ahl-nost?)

98. Could I have my salad without onions?
Може ли да получа салатата си без лук?
(Moh-zheh lee dah poh-loo-chah sah-lah-tah-tah see behz look?)

99. Are there any daily specials?
Имате ли дневни специалитети?
(Ee-mah-teh lee dnehv-nee speh-tsee-ah-lee-teh-tee?)

> **Fun Fact:** Bulgaria is the birthplace of the Cyrillic alphabet, which was developed in the 9th century AD.

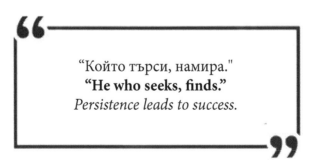

"Който търси, намира."
"He who seeks, finds."
Persistence leads to success.

100. Can I get a side of extra sauce?
Мога ли да получа малко допълнителен сос?
(Moh-gah lee dah poh-loo-chah mahl-koh doh-puhl-nee-teh-len sohs?)

101. I'd like a glass of red/white wine, please.
Бих искал чаша червено/бяло вино, моля.
(Beeh ees-kahl chah-shah chehr-veh-noh/byah-loh vee-noh, moh-lyah.)

102. Could you bring the bill, please?
Можете ли да ми донесете сметката, моля?
(Moh-zheh-teh lee dah mee doh-ne-seh-teh smeh-tkah-tah, moh-lyah?)

Allergies and Intolerances

103. I have a dairy allergy. Is the sauce dairy-free?
Алергичен съм към млечни продукти. Без млечни ли е сосът?
(Ah-lehr-gee-chen sum kuhm mlehch-nee proh-dook-tee. Behz mlehch-nee lee eh soh-suht?)

104. Does this contain any seafood? I have an allergy.
Съдържа ли това морски продукти? Алергичен съм.
(Suh-dur-zhah lee toh-vah mohr-skee proh-dook-tee? Ah-lehr-gee-chen sum.)

105. I can't eat anything with soy. Is that an issue?
Не мога да ям нищо със соя. Проблем ли е това?
(Neh moh-gah dah yahm nee-shtoh suhs soh-yah. Proh-blem lee eh toh-vah?)

106.   I'm lactose intolerant, so no dairy, please.
       **Непоносимост имам към лактоза, така че моля, без
       млечни продукти.**
       *(Neh-poh-noh-see-mohst ee-mahm kuhm lahk-toh-zah, tah-kah
       cheh moh-lyah, behz mlehch-nee proh-dook-tee.)*

107.   Is there an option for those with nut allergies?
       Има ли опция за хора с алергия към ядки?
       *(Ee-mah lee op-tsee-yah zah hoh-rah s ah-lehr-gee-yah kuhm
       yahd-kee?)*

108.   I'm following a vegan diet. Is that possible?
       Спазвам веганска диета. Възможно ли е това?
       *(Spahz-vahm veh-gahn-skah dee-eh-tah. Vuhz-mohzh-noh lee eh
       toh-vah?)*

> **Cultural Insight:** The predominant religion in Bulgaria
> is Eastern Orthodox Christianity, influencing many
> cultural traditions and holidays.

109.   Is this dish suitable for someone with allergies?
       Подходящо ли е това ястие за хора с алергии?
       *(Pohd-hoh-dyah-shoh lee eh toh-vah yah-stee-eh zah hoh-rah s
       ah-lehr-gee-ee?)*

110.   I'm trying to avoid dairy. Any dairy-free options?
       **Опитвам се да избегна млечни продукти. Има ли опции
       без млечни?**
       *(Oh-pee-tvahm seh dah eez-behg-nah mlehch-nee proh-dook-tee.
       Ee-mah lee op-tsee-ee behz mlehch-nee?)*

111.   I have a shellfish allergy. Is it safe to order seafood?
       **Алергичен съм към мекотели. Безопасно ли е да поръчам
       морски продукти?**
       *(Ah-lehr-gee-chen sum kuhm meh-koh-teh-lee. Behz-oh-pahs-noh
       lee eh dah poh-ruh-chahm mohr-skee proh-dook-tee.)*

112. Can you make this gluten-free?
Можете ли да го приготвите без глутен?
(Moh-zheh-teh lee dah goh pree-goh-tvee-teh behz gloo-ten?)

Language Learning Tip: Record Your Voice - This helps in improving your pronunciation.

Specific Dietary Requests

113. I prefer my food without cilantro.
Предпочитам храната си без кориандър.
(Prehd-poh-chee-tahm khrah-nah-tah see behz koh-ree-and-uhr.)

114. Could I have the dressing on the side?
Може ли дресингът да е отделно?
(Moh-zheh lee dreh-seeng-uht dah eh oht-dehl-noh?)

115. Can you make it vegan-friendly?
Можете ли да го приготвите вегански?
(Moh-zheh-teh lee dah goh pree-goh-tvee-teh veh-gahn-skee?)

116. I'd like extra vegetables with my main course.
Бих искал допълнителни зеленчуци към основното ястие.
(Beeh ees-kahl doh-puhl-nee-tehl-nee zeh-lehn-choo-tsee kuhm ohs-nohv-noh-toh yah-stee-eh.)

117. Is this suitable for someone on a keto diet?
Подходящо ли е това за някого на кето диета?
(Pohd-hoh-dyah-shoh lee eh toh-vah zah nyah-koh-goh nah keh-toh dee-eh-tah?)

118. I prefer my food with less oil, please.
Предпочитам храната си с по-малко олио, моля.
(Prehd-poh-chee-tahm khrah-nah-tah see s poh-mahl-koh oh-lee-oh, moh-lyah.)

119. Is this dish suitable for vegetarians?
Подходящо ли е това ястие за вегетарианци?
(Pohd-hoh-dyah-shoh lee eh toh-vah yah-stee-eh zah veh-geh-tah-ree-ahn-tsee?)

120. I'm on a low-carb diet. What would you recommend?
Спазвам диета с ниско съдържание на въглехидрати. Какво бихте препоръчали?
(Spahz-vahm dee-eh-tah s nees-koh suh-duhr-zhah-nee-eh nah vuh-gleh-hee-drah-tee. Kahk-voh bihsh-teh preh-poh-ruh-chah-lee?)

> **Fun Fact:** Bulgaria is known for its yogurt, which contains a unique bacteria called Lactobacillus bulgaricus.

121. Is the bread here gluten-free?
Безглутенов ли е хлябът тук?
(Behz-gloo-teh-nov lee eh khlyah-buht took?)

122. I'm watching my sugar intake. Any sugar-free desserts?
Внимавам за приема на захар. Имате ли беззахарни десерти?
(Vnee-mah-vahm zah pree-eh-mah nah zah-hahr. Ee-mah-teh lee behz-zah-hahr-nee deh-sehr-tee?)

> **Travel Story:** In the ancient city of Plovdiv, amidst Roman ruins, a tour guide said, "Старият град крие много истории" (The old city hides many stories), igniting a sense of mystery and history.

Compliments

123.   This meal is delicious!
       Това ястие е вкусно!
       (Toh-vah yah-stee-eh eh vkoos-noh!)

> **Fun Fact:** Bulgaria produces about 70% of the world's
> rose oil, an essential ingredient in perfumery.

124.   The flavors in this dish are amazing.
       Вкусовете в това ястие са невероятни.
       *(Vkoos-oh-veh-teh v toh-vah yah-stee-eh sah
       neh-veh-roh-yat-nee.)*

125.   I love the presentation of the food.
       Обожавам поднасянето на храната.
       *(Oh-boh-zhah-vahm pohd-nah-syah-neh-toh nah
       khrah-nah-tah.)*

126.   This dessert is outstanding!
       Този десерт е изключителен!
       (Toh-zee deh-sehrt eh eez-kloo-chee-teh-len!)

127.   The service here is exceptional.
       Обслужването тук е изключително.
       (Ob-sloo-zh-vah-neh-toh took eh eez-kloo-chee-tel-noh.)

> **Language Learning Tip:** Keep a Vocabulary Diary -
> Write down new words you learn each day.

128.   The chef deserves praise for this dish.
       Главният готвач заслужава похвала за това ястие.
       *(Glahv-nee-yat goht-vahch zah-sloo-zhah-vah poh-khva-lah zah
       toh-vah yah-stee-eh.)*

129. I'm impressed by the quality of the ingredients.
Впечатлен съм от качеството на съставките.
*(Vpeh-chaht-lehn sum oht kahch-es-tvoh-toh nah
suhs-tahv-kee-teh.)*

130. The atmosphere in this restaurant is wonderful.
Атмосферата в този ресторант е прекрасна.
*(Aht-mohs-feh-rah-tah v toh-zee rehs-toh-rahnt eh
preh-kras-nah.)*

131. Everything we ordered was perfect.
Всичко, което поръчахме, беше перфектно.
*(Vseech-koh, koh-eh-toh poh-ruh-chahh-meh, beh-sheh
pehr-fek-t-noh.)*

Compaints

132. The food is cold. Can you reheat it?
Храната е студена. Можете ли да я загреете отново?
*(Krah-nah-tah eh stoo-deh-nah. Moh-zheh-teh lee dah yah
zah-greh-eh-teh oht-noh-voh?)*

> **Fun Fact:** The traditional Bulgarian musical instrument
> is the gaida, a type of bagpipe.

133. This dish is too spicy for me.
Това ястие е твърде люто за мен.
(Toh-vah yah-stee-eh eh tvuhr-deh lyoo-toh zah mehn.)

134. The portion size is quite small.
Размерът на порцията е доста малък.
(Rahz-meh-ruht nah pohr-tsee-yah-tah eh dohs-tah mah-luhk.)

135. There's a hair in my food.
Има косъм в храната ми.
(*Ee-mah koh-suhm v khrah-nah-tah mee.*)

136. I'm not satisfied with the service.
Не съм доволен от обслужването.
(*Neh sum doh-voh-len oht ob-sloo-zh-vah-neh-toh.*)

137. The soup is lukewarm.
Супата е хладка.
(*Soo-pah-tah eh khlahd-kah.*)

138. The sauce on this dish is too salty.
Сосът на това ястие е твърде солен.
(*Soh-suht nah toh-vah yah-stee-eh eh tvur-deh soh-len.*)

> **Idiomatic Expression:** "Пускам си на кафето."
> Meaning: "To take one's time, relax."
> (Literal translation: "To let oneself to the coffee.")

139. The dessert was a bit disappointing.
Десертът беше малко разочароващ.
(*Deh-sehrt-uht beh-sheh mahl-koh rah-zoh-chah-roh-va-sht.*)

140. I ordered this dish, but you brought me something else.
Поръчах това ястие, но ми донесохте нещо друго.
(*Poh-ruh-chahh toh-vah yah-stee-eh, noh mee doh-neh-soh-shteh neh-shtoh droo-goh.*)

141. The food took a long time to arrive.
Храната отне много време да пристигне.
(*Khrah-nah-tah oht-neh mnoh-goh vreh-meh dah prees-teeg-neh.*)

Specific Dish Feedback

142. The steak is overcooked.
Стекът е преготвен.
(Steh-kuht eh preh-goh-tvehn.)

> **Fun Fact:** The world's oldest gold treasure, dating back over 6,000 years, was discovered in Varna.

143. This pasta is undercooked.
Тази паста е недоварена.
(Tah-zee pahs-tah eh neh-doh-vah-reh-nah.)

144. The fish tastes off. Is it fresh?
Рибата има странен вкус. Свежа ли е?
(Ree-bah-tah ee-mah strah-nen vkus. Sveh-zhah lee eh?)

145. The salad dressing is too sweet.
Дресингът на салатата е твърде сладък.
(Dreh-seen-guht nah sah-lah-tah-tah eh tvur-deh slah-duhk.)

146. The rice is underseasoned.
Оризът е недостатъчно подправен.
(Oh-rees-uht eh neh-doh-stah-tuhch-noh pohd-prah-vehn.)

> **Language Learning Tip:** Set Realistic Goals - Such as learning ten new words a day.

147. The dessert lacks flavor.
На десерта липсва вкус.
(Nah deh-sehr-tah leeps-vah vkus.)

148. The vegetables are overcooked.
Зеленчуците са преварени.
(Zeh-lehn-choo-tsee-teh sah preh-vah-reh-nee.)

149. The pizza crust is burnt.
Корала на пицата е изгоряла.
(Koh-rah-tah nah pee-tsah-tah eh eez-goh-ryah-lah.)

> **Travel Story:** At a lively folk festival in Koprivshtitsa, a dancer exclaimed, "Танцът е език без думи" (Dance is a language without words), capturing the essence of their vibrant culture.

150. The burger is dry.
Бургерът е сух.
(Boor-gehr-uht eh sooh.)

151. The fries are too greasy.
Пържените картофи са твърде мазни.
(Pur-zheh-nee-teh kar-toh-fee sah tvur-deh mahz-nee.)

152. The soup is too watery.
Супата е твърде водниста.
(Soo-pah-tah eh tvur-deh vod-nees-tah.)

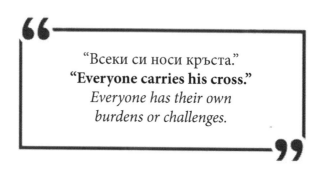

"Всеки си носи кръста."
"Everyone carries his cross."
*Everyone has their own
burdens or challenges.*

Word Search Puzzle: Eating & Dining

RESTAURANT
РЕСТОРАНТ
MENU
МЕНЮ
APPETIZER
ПРЕДЯСТИЕ
VEGETARIAN
ВЕГЕТАРИАНЕЦ
ALLERGY
АЛЕРГИЯ
VEGAN
ВЕГАН
SPECIAL
СПЕЦИАЛЕН
DESSERT
ДЕСЕРТ
SERVICE
ОБСЛУЖВАНЕ
CHEF
ГЛАВЕН ГОТВАЧ
INGREDIENTS
СЪСТАВКИ
ATMOSPHERE
АТМОСФЕРА
PERFECT
ПЕРФЕКТЕН

```
A E I B D Z B Z J L Y M I L S
Ц В В А А Л Е Р Г И Я Т Е Е L
E E S T N E I D E R G N I N A
Н Г C V Y B U V C D V W J P U
А А M E A T M I M O W S P Y Z
И Н Р Е С Т О Р А Н Т E G M M
P B L W R E U P G N T R T V S
A N K L B F X P V I E A K P A
T D Y P N N E Q Z L J W E F N
E L N D L J E E L U J C S V E
Г L P N Y K R A Z J I X H C V
E И Т С Я Д Е Р П А В Y I E V
B Z O T H R G A L L J V Г A F
V Н Е Л А И Ц Е П C R А Л L D
L E L C Q X C E T E D Г А L C
И N G N Y S D V S R O P B B V
Q K G A A I E D A T E T E U X
T W B U N I P S B T V S H J L
P P I A P F R A N E H Y S W C
E В Е M T А Ч A H M I O M E D
C E R R X C R G T Q J H B T D
E Y E F F U ъ X G E J A В А П
Д N H E A E C C H B G P V J E
C F P T M T C L M A N E Y T P
S M S J E N T T H M W O V Z Ф
О Е О О Н О Б C Л У Ж В А Н Е
R S M R Ю А Т М О С Ф Е Р А К
W E T S D J M G Q Z F M U J T
T E A Z L C O U P F N T W M E
V T Q N X Y Q F S S V F N H H
```

Correct Answers:

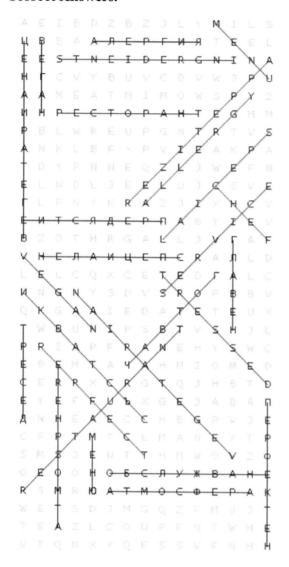

TRAVEL & TRANSPORTATION

- ASKING FOR DIRECTIONS -
- BUYING TICKETS FOR TRANSPORTATION -
- INQUIRING ABOUT TRAVEL-RELATED INFORMATION -

Directions

153. How do I get to the nearest bus stop?
Как да стигна до най-близката автобусна спирка?
(Kahk dah stee-gnah doh nigh-bleez-kah-tah ahv-toh-boos-nah speer-kah?)

> **Fun Fact:** John Atanasoff, a Bulgarian-American, is credited with inventing the first digital electronic computer.

154. Can you show me the way to the train station?
Можете ли да ми покажете пътя до гарата?
(Moh-zheh-teh lee dah mee poh-kah-zheh-teh puht-yah doh gah-rah-tah?)

155. Is there a map of the city center?
Има ли карта на центъра на града?
(Ee-mah lee kahr-tah nah tsehn-tuhr-ah nah grah-dah?)

156. Which street leads to the airport?
Коя улица води до летището?
(Koh-yah oo-lee-tsah voh-dee doh leh-teesh-teh-toh?)

157. Where is the nearest taxi stand?
Къде е най-близкият таксиметрова площадка?
(Kuh-deh eh nigh-bleez-kee-yat tahk-see-meh-troh-vah ploh-shahd-kah?)

> **Travel Story:** In the Rila Monastery, a monk shared, "Тук времето спира" (Here, time stops), highlighting the timeless spirituality of the place.

158. How can I find the hotel from here?
Как мога да намеря хотела оттук?
(Kahk moh-gah dah nah-meh-ryah hoh-teh-lah oht-took?)

> **Fun Fact:** The oldest worked gold in the world was found in the Varna Necropolis.

159. What's the quickest route to the museum?
Какъв е най-бързият маршрут до музея?
(Kah-kuhv eh nigh-bur-zee-yat mahr-shroot doh moo-zeh-yah?)

160. Is there a pedestrian path to the beach?
Има ли пешеходен път към плажа?
(Ee-mah lee peh-sheh-hoh-den puht kuhm plah-zhah?)

161. Can you point me towards the city square?
Можете ли да ме насочите към градския площад?
(Moh-zheh-teh lee dah meh nah-soh-chee-teh kuhm grahd-skee-yah ploh-shtahd?)

> **Idiomatic Expression:** "Слагам ти ръка на рамото." - Meaning: "I guarantee or vouch for you."
> (Literal translation: "I put my hand on your shoulder.")

162. How do I find the trailhead for the hiking trail?
Как да намеря началото на туристическата пътека?
(Kahk dah nah-meh-ryah nah-chah-loh-toh nah too-rees-tee-ches-kah-tah puh-teh-kah?)

> **Fun Fact:** Bulgaria has an impressive number of opera singers renowned worldwide.

Ticket Purchase

163. How much is a one-way ticket to downtown?
Колко струва билет в една посока до центъра?
(Kohl-koh stroo-vah bee-let v ed-nah poh-soh-kah doh tsehn-tuh-rah?)

164. Are there any discounts for students?
Има ли отстъпки за студенти?
(Ee-mah lee oht-stuhp-kee zah stoo-den-tee?)

> **Language Learning Tip:** Read Bulgarian Newspapers Online - For modern vocabulary and real-life usage.

165. What's the price of a monthly bus pass?
Колко струва месечен абонамент за автобус?
(Kohl-koh stroo-vah meh-seh-chen ah-boh-nah-ment zah ahv-toh-boos?)

166. Can I buy a metro ticket for a week?
Мога ли да купя седмичен билет за метрото?
(Moh-gah lee dah koo-pyah sed-mee-chen bee-let zah meh-troh-toh?)

167. How do I get a refund for a canceled flight?
Как да получа възстановяване на пари за отменен полет?
(Kahk dah poh-loo-chah vuhz-stoh-noh-tyah-vah-neh nah pah-ree zah oht-meh-nen poh-let?)

> **Fun Fact:** The Bulgarian army has never lost a single flag in battle.

168. Is it cheaper to purchase tickets online or at the station?
По-евтино ли е да купите билети онлайн или на гарата?
(Poh-ehv-tee-noh lee eh dah koo-pee-teh bee-let-ee ohn-line eely nah gah-rah-tah?)

169. Can I upgrade my bus ticket to first class?
Мога ли да променя моя автобусен билет до първи клас?
(Moh-gah lee dah proh-meh-nyah moh-yah ahv-toh-boo-sen bee-let doh pur-vee klahs?)

170. Are there any promotions for weekend train travel?
Има ли промоции за пътуване с влак през уикенда?
(Ee-mah lee proh-moh-tsee-eh zah puh-too-vah-neh s vlak prehz oo-ee-ken-dah?)

171. Is there a night bus to the city center?
Има ли нощен автобус до центъра?
(Ee-mah lee nohsh-ten ahv-toh-boos doh tsehn-tuh-rah?)

> **Idiomatic Expression:** "На кривия пазар." -
> Meaning: "In a crooked situation or in trouble."
> (Literal translation: "At the crooked market.")

172. What's the cost of a one-day tram pass?
Колко струва еднодневен билет за трамвая?
(Kohl-koh stroo-vah ed-noh-dneh-ven bee-let zah trahm-vah-yah?)

> **Fun Fact:** Bulgaria was the sixth country in the world to have an astronaut in space.

Travel Info

173.   What's the weather forecast for tomorrow?
       Каква е прогнозата за времето за утре?
       (Kahk-vah eh proh-gnoh-zah-tah zah vreh-meh-toh zah oo-treh?)

174.   Are there any guided tours of the historical sites?
       Има ли екскурзоводски обиколки на историческите забележителности?
       (Ee-mah lee ehk-skur-zoh-vod-skee oh-bee-kohl-kee nah ees-toh-ree-chehs-kee-teh zah-beh-leh-zhee-tehl-nos-tee?)

175.   Can you recommend a good local restaurant for dinner?
       Можете ли да препоръчате добър местен ресторант за вечеря?
       (Moh-zheh-teh lee dah preh-poh-ruh-chah-teh doh-bur meh-sten rehs-toh-rahn-t zah veh-cheh-ryah?)

176.   How do I get to the famous landmarks in town?
       Как да стигна до известните забележителности в града?
       (Kahk dah stee-gnah doh eez-vehst-nee-teh zah-beh-leh-zhee-tehl-nos-tee v grah-dah?)

177.   Is there a visitor center at the airport?
       Има ли информационен център на летището?
       (Ee-mah lee een-for-mah-tsee-on-en tsehn-tuhr nah leh-tee-shteh-toh?)

178.   What's the policy for bringing pets on the train?
       Каква е политиката за носене на домашни любимци във влака?
       (Kahk-vah eh poh-lee-tee-kah-tah zah noh-seh-neh nah doh-mahsh-nee lyoo-beem-tsee vuhv vlah-kah?)

179. Are there any discounts for disabled travelers?
Има ли отстъпки за пътуващи с увреждания?
(Ee-mah lee oht-stuhp-kee zah puh-too-vah-shtee s oo-vrehzhdah-nee-yah?)

> **Idiomatic Expression:** "Да ти мине филмът." -
> Meaning: "To lose consciousness or faint."
> (Literal translation: "For your film to pass.")

180. Can you provide information about local festivals?
Можете ли да дадете информация за местни фестивали?
(Moh-zheh-teh lee dah dah-deh-teh een-for-mah-tsee-yah zah mehst-nee fehs-tee-vah-lee?)

181. Is there Wi-Fi available on long bus journeys?
Има ли Wi-Fi на дългите автобусни пътувания?
(Ee-mah lee wee-fee nah duhl-gee-teh ahv-toh-boos-nee puh-too-vah-nee-yah?)

> **Fun Fact:** The Rila Monastery, a UNESCO World
> Heritage site, is a must-visit for its stunning architecture
> and art.

182. Where can I rent a bicycle for exploring the city?
Къде мога да наема колело за разглеждане на града?
(Kuh-deh moh-gah dah nah-eh-mah koh-leh-loh zah rahz-glehzh-dah-neh nah grah-dah?)

> **Travel Story:** While hiking in the Pirin Mountains, a
> fellow traveler pointed out, "Всяка стъпка разкрива
> нови гледки" (Every step reveals new views),
> emphasizing the beauty of Bulgaria's natural landscapes.

Getting Around by Public Transportation

183. Which bus should I take to reach the city center?
Кой автобус трябва да взема, за да стигна до центъра на града?
(Koy ahv-toh-boos tryab-vah dah vzeh-mah, zah dah stee-gnah doh tsehn-tuh-rah nah grah-dah?)

184. Can I buy a day pass for unlimited rides?
Мога ли да купя дневен билет за неограничени пътувания?
(Moh-gah lee dah koo-pyah dheh-vehn bee-let zah neh-oh-grah-nee-cheh-nee puht-oo-vah-nee-yah?)

185. Is there a metro station within walking distance?
Има ли метростанция на разстояние за пешеходци?
(Ee-mah lee meh-troh-stahn-tsee-yah nah rahz-stoh-yah-nee-eh zah peh-sheh-hohd-tsee?)

186. How do I transfer between different bus lines?
Как да се прехвърля между различните автобусни линии?
(Kahk dah seh prehvur-lyah mezh-doo rahz-leechn-ee-teh ahv-toh-boos-nee lee-nee-ee?)

187. Are there any discounts for senior citizens?
Има ли отстъпки за възрастни хора?
(Ee-mah lee oht-stuhp-kee zah vuhz-rahst-nee hoh-rah?)

188. What's the last bus/train for the night?
Кой е последният автобус/влак за вечерта?
(Koy eh poh-sleh-dee-yat ahv-toh-boos/vlahk zah veh-chehr-tah?)

189. Are there any express buses to [destination]?
Има ли експресни автобуси до [дестинацията]?
(Ee-mah lee ehk-spreh-snee ahv-toh-boo-see doh [deh-stee-nah-tsee-ah-tah]?)

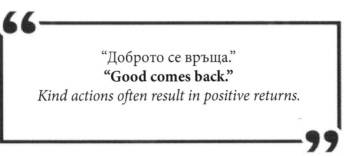

"Доброто се връща."
"Good comes back."
Kind actions often result in positive returns.

190. Do trams run on weekends as well?
Трамваите ли се движат и през уикендите?
(Trahm-vah-ee-teh lee seh dvee-zhut ee prehz oo-ee-ken-dee-teh?)

> **Fun Fact:** Bulgarian is a South Slavic language with over 12 million speakers worldwide.

191. Can you recommend a reliable taxi service?
Можете ли да препоръчате надеждна таксиметрова услуга?
(Moh-zheh-teh lee dah preh-poh-ruh-chah-teh nah-dezh-dnah tahk-see-meh-troh-vah oos-loo-gah?)

192. What's the fare for a one-way ticket to the suburbs?
Колко струва билет в една посока до предградията?
(Kohl-koh stroo-vah bee-let v ed-nah poh-soh-kah doh prehd-grah-dee-yah-tah?)

> **Travel Story:** At a quaint café in Veliko Tarnovo, a local mused, "Кафето е повече от напитка" (Coffee is more than a drink), underlining the cultural significance of coffee in Bulgarian daily life.

Navigating the Airport

193. Where can I locate the baggage claim area?
      Къде мога да намеря зоната за получаване на багаж?
      (Kuh-deh moh-gah dah nah-meh-ryah zoh-nah-tah zah poh-loo-chah-vah-neh nah bah-gahzh?)

194. Is there a currency exchange counter in the terminal?
      Има ли бюро за обмяна на валута в терминала?
      (Ee-mah lee byoo-roh zah ohb-myah-nah nah vah-loo-tah v tehr-mee-nah-lah?)

      > **Idiomatic Expression:** "Без да мигне." -
      > Meaning: "Without hesitation."
      > (Literal translation: "Without blinking.")

195. Are there any pet relief areas for service animals?
      Има ли зони за облекчение на домашни любимци?
      (Ee-mah lee zoh-nee zah oh-blehk-cheh-neh-nah doh-mahsh-nee lyoo-beem-tsee?)

196. How early can I go through security?
      Колко рано мога да минавам през сигурността?
      (Kohl-koh rah-noh moh-gah dah mee-nah-vahm prehz see-goor-nos-tah?)

197. What's the procedure for boarding the aircraft?
      Каква е процедурата за качване на самолета?
      (Kahk-vah eh proh-tseh-doo-rah-tah zah kahch-vah-neh nah sah-moh-leh-tah?)

198. Can I use mobile boarding passes?
      Мога ли да използвам мобилни карти за качване?
      (Moh-gah lee dah eez-pohlz-vahm moh-beel-nee kar-tee zah kahch-vah-neh?)

199. Are there any restaurants past security?
Има ли ресторанти след зоната за сигурност?
(Ee-mah lee rehs-toh-rahn-tee slehd zoh-nah-tah zah see-goor-nos-t?)

200. What's the airport's Wi-Fi password?
Каква е паролата за Wi-Fi на летището?
(Kahk-vah eh pah-roh-lah-tah zah Vee-Fee nah leh-tee-shteh-toh?)

201. Can I bring duty-free items on board?
Мога ли да взема безмитни стоки на борда?
(Moh-gah lee dah vzeh-mah behz-meet-nee stoh-kee nah bohr-dah?)

202. Is there a pharmacy at the airport?
Има ли аптека на летището?
(Ee-mah lee ahp-teh-kah nah leh-tee-shteh-toh?)

Traveling by Car

203. How do I pay tolls on the highway?
Как се плащат таксите на магистралата?
(Kahk seh plahsh-taht tahk-see-teh nah mah-gee-strah-lah-tah?)

204. Where can I find a car wash nearby?
Къде мога да намеря автомивка наблизо?
(Kuh-deh moh-gah dah nah-meh-ryah ahv-toh-meevkah nah-blee-zoh?)

205. Are there electric vehicle charging stations?
Има ли зарядни станции за електрически автомобили?
(Ee-mah lee zah-ryad-nee stahn-tsee zah eh-lehk-tree-chehs-kee ahv-toh-moh-bee-lee?)

206. Can I rent a GPS navigation system with the car?
Мога ли да наема GPS навигация с колата?
(Moh-gah lee dah nah-eh-mah Jee-Pee-Ess nah-vee-gah-tsee-ah s koh-lah-tah?)

207. What's the cost of parking in the city center?
Колко струва паркирането в центъра на града?
(Kohl-koh stroo-vah pahr-kee-rah-neh-toh v tsehn-tuh-rah nah grah-dah?)

208. Do I need an international driving permit?
Трябва ли ми международен шофьорски лиценз?
(Tryab-vah lee mee mezh-doo-nah-roh-den shohf-yor-skee lee-tsehnz?)

209. Is roadside assistance available?
Има ли помощ на пътя?
(Ee-mah lee poh-mosht nah puht-yah?)

210. Are there any traffic cameras on this route?
Има ли камери за наблюдение по този маршрут?
(Ee-mah lee kah-meh-ree zah nahb-lyoo-deh-nee-eh poh toh-zee mahr-shroot?)

211. Can you recommend a reliable mechanic?
Можете ли да препоръчате надежден механик?
(Moh-zheh-teh lee dah preh-poh-ruh-chah-teh nah-dezh-den meh-hah-neek?)

212. What's the speed limit in residential areas?
Какъв е скоростният лимит в жилищните райони?
(Kah-kuv eh skoh-rohst-nee-yat lee-meet v zhee-leesht-nee-teh ray-oh-nee?)

Airport Transfers and Shuttles

213. Where is the taxi stand located at the airport?
Къде е таксиметровата спирка на летището?
(Kuh-deh eh tahk-see-meh-troh-vah-tah speer-kah nah leh-tee-shteh-toh?)

214. Do airport shuttles run 24/7?
Работят ли летищните шатъли непрекъснато?
(Rah-boh-tyat lee leh-tee-sht-nee-teh shah-tuh-lee neh-preh-kuhs-nah-toh?)

> **Idiomatic Expression:** "Всичко е ток и жица." -
> Meaning: "It's very complicated or tricky."
> (Literal translation: "Everything is wire and cable.")

215. How long does it take to reach downtown by taxi?
Колко време отнема да стигнем до центъра на града с такси?
(Kohl-koh vreh-meh oht-neh-mah dah stee-gnehm doh tsehn-tuh-rah nah grah-dah s tahk-see?)

216. Is there a designated pick-up area for ride-sharing services?
Има ли определено място за прибиране от услуги за споделено пътуване?
(Ee-mah lee oh-preh-deh-leh-noh myahs-toh zah pree-bee-rah-neh oht oos-loo-ghee zah spoh-deh-leh-noh puht-oo-vah-neh?)

217. Can I book a shuttle in advance?
Мога ли да резервирам шатъл предварително?
(Moh-gah lee dah reh-zehr-vee-rahm shah-tuhl prehd-vah-ree-tehl-noh?)

> **Fun Fact:** Bulgaria ranks third in Europe in biodiversity, with several national parks and nature reserves.

218. Do hotels offer free shuttle service to the airport?
Предлагат ли хотелите безплатен трансфер до летището?
(Preh-dlah-gaht lee hoh-teh-lee-teh behz-plah-ten trahns-fehr doh leh-tee-shteh-toh?)

219. What's the rate for a private airport transfer?
Колко струва частен трансфер до летището?
(Kohl-koh stroo-vah chah-sten trahns-fehr doh leh-tee-shteh-toh?)

220. Are there any public buses connecting to the airport?
Има ли обществени автобуси, които отиват до летището?
(Ee-mah lee obsh-tehs-tveh-nee ahv-toh-boo-see, koh-ee-toh oh-tee-vat doh leh-tee-shteh-toh?)

221. Can you recommend a reliable limousine service?
Можете ли да препоръчате надеждна лимузинова услуга?
(Moh-zheh-teh lee dah preh-poh-ruh-chah-teh nah-dezh-dnah lee-moo-zee-noh-vah oos-loo-gah?)

222. Is there an airport shuttle for early morning flights?
Има ли трансфер до летището за ранни полети?
(Ee-mah lee trahns-fehr doh leh-tee-shteh-toh zah rah-nee poh-leh-tee?)

Traveling with Luggage

223. Can I check my bags at this train station?
Мога ли да регистрирам багажа си на тази гара?
(Moh-gah lee dah reh-gee-stree-rahm bah-gah-zhah see nah tah-zee gah-rah?)

224. Where can I find baggage carts in the airport?
Къде мога да намеря колички за багаж на летището?
(Kuh-deh moh-gah dah nah-meh-ryah koh-leech-kee zah bah-gahzh nah leh-tee-shteh-toh?)

> **Fun Fact:** Rich in folklore, Bulgaria celebrates many ancient customs and dances, like the famous fire dance, Nestinarstvo.

225. Are there weight limits for checked baggage?
Има ли теглови ограничения за регистрирания багаж?
(Ee-mah lee teh-gloh-vee oh-grah-nee-cheh-nee-yah zah reh-gee-stree-rah-nee-yah bah-gahzh?)

226. Can I carry my backpack as a personal item?
Мога ли да нося раницата си като личен багаж?
(Moh-gah lee dah noh-syah rah-nee-tsah-tah see kah-toh lee-chen bah-gahzh?)

227. What's the procedure for oversized luggage?
Каква е процедурата за голям багаж?
(Kahk-vah eh proh-tseh-doo-rah-tah zah goh-lyahm bah-gahzh?)

228. Can I bring a stroller on the bus?
Мога ли да взема детска количка на автобуса?
(Moh-gah lee dah vze-mah deht-skah koh-leech-kah nah ahv-toh-boo-sah?)

229. Are there lockers for storing luggage at the airport?
Има ли сейфове за съхранение на багаж на летището?
(Ee-mah lee say-foh-veh zah suh-hrah-neh-nee-eh nah bah-gahzh nah leh-tee-shteh-toh?)

> **Fun Fact:** Bulgarian cuisine is known for its variety of salads, pastries, and dairy products.

230. How do I label my luggage with contact information?
Как да маркирам багажа си с контактна информация?
(Kahk dah mahr-kee-rahm bah-gah-zhah see s kohn-tahkt-nah een-for-mah-tsee-yah?)

231. Is there a lost and found office at the train station?
Има ли офис за изгубени вещи на гарата?
(Ee-mah lee oh-fees zah eez-goo-beh-nee veh-shtee nah gah-rah-tah?)

> **Idiomatic Expression:** "Това не е за моята кола." - Meaning: "That's not my thing or not suitable for me." (Literal translation: "This is not for my cart.")

232. Can I carry fragile items in my checked bags?
Мога ли да пренасям крехки вещи в регистрирания си багаж?
(Moh-gah lee dah preh-nah-syahm kreh-hee veh-shtee v reh-gee-stree-rah-nee-yah see bah-gahzh?)

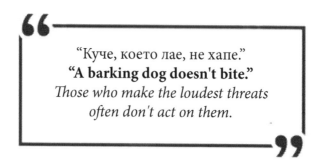

"Куче, което лае, не хапе."
"A barking dog doesn't bite."
Those who make the loudest threats often don't act on them.

Word Search Puzzle: Travel & Transportation

AIRPORT
ЛЕТИЩЕ
BUS
АВТОБУС
TAXI
ТАКСИ
TICKET
БИЛЕТ
MAP
КАРТА
CAR
КОЛА
METRO
МЕТРО
BICYCLE
КОЛЕЛО
DEPARTURE
ОТПЪТУВАНЕ
ARRIVAL
ПРИСТИГАНЕ
ROAD
ПЪТ
PLATFORM
ПЕРОН
STATION
СТАНЦИЯ
TERMINAL
ТЕРМИНАЛ

```
U G L U Z A C H O P E П J F O
K A D B N У T R Y H F N L J V
O M X E Б O K P Y E C X F K C
O Y R O H X I M A K Q G F M R
K H T П B A V T E K S H W B L
P B G Ъ N P B P A T K X T C M
A D D T R B L У N T P I I R F
N I P V U A L K T N S O C K K
A Q Y L T A X I B Ъ J W K H W
D G P F W I L Y I J П S E C M
B E O V I V K L C I Y T T W P
Z R I F H O A Z Y P A M O N B
M D O W Л N T R C F T Z K C N
M P Y E I V G F L S J A M M U
R K Л M U V L U E R J C K F H
A O R W X I T R O P R I A C B
C E R U T R A P E D J D P N И
T F R F I J V R M Q G P L H O
C W G W E B Б O T P L W A Я C
E F W P M И Q D A E J E V И I
C Щ V R Л S A M E T R O I Ц H
U M И E O Л Y E O W H Z R H K
Z E T T O A T S P I L R R A B
Y E L K E D D E L O W L A T I
B A T V S Л O P U N Z A F C J
X X H V U П P И C T И Г A H E
Z A Z A B S Q B K H I D Q N S
J E M K H J X T K F Q K Z U U
W X T E P M И H A Л F Z V T Y
U C K Z W W W Q C O S V R S H
```

Correct Answers:

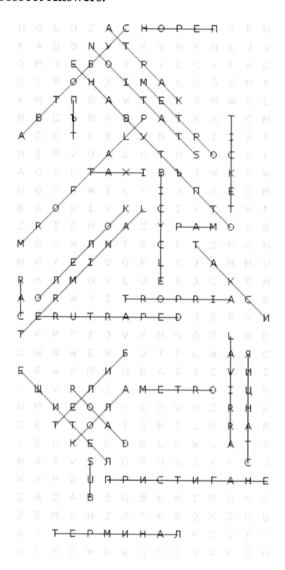

ACCOMMODATIONS

- CHECKING INTO A HOTEL -
- ASKING ABOUT ROOM AMENITIES -
- REPORTING ISSUES OR MAKING REQUESTS -

Hotel Check-In

233. I have a reservation under [Name].
Имам резервация на име [Име].
(*Ee-mahm reh-zer-va-tsee-yah nah ee-meh [Ee-meh].*)

234. Can I see some identification, please?
Мога ли да видя някакъв документ за самоличност, моля?
(*Moh-gah lee dah vee-dyah nyah-kah-kuhv doh-koo-ment zah sah-moh-leech-nost, moh-lyah?*)

235. What time is check-in/check-out?
Кога е настаняването/напускането?
(*Koh-gah eh nah-stahn-yah-vah-neh-toh/nah-poos-kah-neh-toh?*)

236. Is breakfast included in the room rate?
Включена ли е закуската в цената на стаята?
(*Vkloo-cheh-nah lee eh zah-koos-kah-tah v tseh-nah-tah nah stah-yah-tah?*)

237. Do you need a credit card for incidentals?
Трябва ли ми кредитна карта за допълнителни разходи?
(*Tryab-vah lee mee kreh-diht-nah kar-tah zah doh-puhl-nee-tehl-nee rahz-hoh-dee?*)

238. May I have a room key, please?
Мога ли да получа ключа на стаята, моля?
(*Moh-gah lee dah poh-loo-chah kloo-chah nah stah-yah-tah, moh-lyah?*)

239. Is there a shuttle service to the airport?
Има ли шатъл услуга до летището?
(*Ee-mah lee shah-tuhl oos-loo-gah doh leh-tee-shteh-toh?*)

240. Could you call a bellhop for assistance?
Можете ли да повикате багажник за помощ?
(*Moh-zheh-teh lee dah poh-vee-kah-teh bah-gahzh-neek zah poh-mosht?*)

> **Fun Fact:** Bulgaria celebrates its liberation from Ottoman rule on March 3rd.

Room Amenities

241. Can I request a non-smoking room?
Мога ли да поискам стая за непушачи?
(*Moh-gah lee dah poh-ees-kahm stah-yah zah neh-poo-shah-chee?*)

242. Is there a mini-fridge in the room?
Има ли мини-хладилник в стаята?
(*Ee-mah lee mee-nee-hlah-deel-neek v stah-yah-tah?*)

243. Do you provide free Wi-Fi access?
Предлагате ли безплатен достъп до Wi-Fi?
(*Preh-dlah-gah-teh lee behz-plah-ten doh-stuhp doh Vee-Fee?*)

244. Can I have an extra pillow or blanket?
Мога ли да получа допълнителна възглавница или одеяло?
(*Moh-gah lee dah poh-loo-chah doh-puhl-nee-tehl-nah vuhz-glahv-nee-tsah eely oh-deh-yah-loh?*)

245. Is there a hairdryer in the bathroom?
Има ли сешоар в банята?
(*Ee-mah lee seh-shoh-ar v bah-nyah-tah?*)

246. What's the TV channel lineup?
Какви са телевизионните канали?
(*Kahk-vee sah teh-leh-vee-zee-on-nee-teh kah-nah-lee?*)

247. Are toiletries like shampoo provided?
Предоставят ли се основни тоалетни принадлежности като шампоан?
(*Preh-doh-stah-vyat lee seh oh-sohv-nee toh-ah-let-nee pree-nah-dlehzh-nos-tee kah-toh shahm-poh-ahn?*)

248. Is room service available 24/7?
Има ли стаен сервиз на разположение денонощно?
(*Ee-mah lee stah-en sehr-veez nah rahz-poh-loh-zheh-nee-eh deh-noh-nosh-noh?*)

> **Fun Fact:** The Seven Rila Lakes in the Rila Mountains are a popular natural tourist attraction.

Reporting Issues

249. There's a problem with the air conditioning.
Има проблем с климатика.
(*Ee-mah proh-blem s klee-mah-tee-kah.*)

250. The shower is not working properly.
Душът не работи правилно.
(*Doosh-uht neh rah-boh-tee prah-veel-noh.*)

251. My room key card isn't functioning.
Ключ-картата ми за стаята не работи.
(*Kloo-eech-kahr-tah-tah mee zah stah-yah-tah neh rah-boh-tee.*)

252. There's a leak in the bathroom.
Има теч в банята.
(*Ee-mah teech v bah-nyah-tah.*)

253. The TV remote is not responding.
Дистанционното за телевизора не работи.
(*Dees-tahn-tsee-on-noh-toh zah teh-leh-vee-zoh-rah neh rah-boh-tee.*)

254. Can you fix the broken light in my room?
Можете ли да поправите счупената лампа в моята стая?
(*Moh-zheh-teh lee dah poh-prah-vee-teh schoo-peh-nah-tah lahmpah v moh-yah-tah stah-yah?*)

255. I need assistance with my luggage.
Трябва ми помощ с багажа ми.
(*Tryab-vah mee poh-mosht s bah-gah-zhah mee.*)

256. There's a strange noise coming from next door.
От съседната стая идва странен шум.
(*Oht suh-sehd-nah-tah stah-yah eed-vah strah-nen shoom.*)

Making Requests

257. Can I have a wake-up call at 7 AM?
Мога ли да получа сутрешен будителен звъняг в 7 сутринта?
(*Moh-gah lee dah poh-loo-chah soo-treh-shehn boo-dee-teh-len zvuhn-yahg v sedum soo-treen-tah?*)

> **Fun Fact:** Bansko is a popular ski resort known internationally, attracting winter sports enthusiasts.

258. Please send extra towels to my room.
Моля, изпратете допълнителни кърпи в стаята ми.
(*Moh-lyah, eez-prah-teh-teh doh-puhl-nee-tehl-nee kur-pee v stah-yah-tah mee.*)

259. Could you arrange a taxi for tomorrow?
Можете ли да организирате такси за утре?
(*Moh-zheh-teh lee dah or-gah-nee-zee-rah-teh tahk-see zah oo-treh?*)

260. I'd like to extend my stay for two more nights.
Искам да удължа престоя си с още две нощи.
(*Ees-kahm dah oo-duhl-zhah preh-stoh-yah see s oh-shteh dveh no-shtee.*)

> **Idiomatic Expression:** "Влизам в час." -
> Meaning: "To get up to date."
> (Literal translation: "I'm entering into the hour.")

261. Is it possible to change my room?
Възможно ли е да сменя стаята си?
(*Vuhz-mohzh-noh lee eh dah smehn-yah stah-yah-tah see?*)

262. Can I have a late check-out at 2 PM?
Мога ли да напусна стаята по-късно в 14 часа?
(*Moh-gah lee dah nah-poos-nah stah-yah-tah poh-kuhs-noh v chet-ee-ree-nah-dtseh-tsaht-sah?*)

263. I need an iron and ironing board.
Трябва ми ютия и дъска за гладене.
(*Tryab-vah mee yoo-tee-yah ee duhs-kah zah glah-deh-neh.*)

264. Could you provide directions to [location]?
Можете ли да ми дадете указания за [място]?
(*Moh-zheh-teh lee dah mee dah-deh-teh oo-kah-zah-nee-yah zah [myah-stoh]?*)

Room Types and Preferences

265. I'd like to book a single room, please.
Искам да резервирам единична стая, моля.
(*Ees-kahm dah reh-zer-vee-rahm eh-dee-neech-nah stah-yah, moh-lyah.*)

266. Do you have any suites available?
Имате ли свободни апартаменти?
(*Ee-mah-teh lee svoh-bod-nee ah-pahr-tah-mehn-tee?*)

267. Is there a room with a view of the city?
Има ли стая с изглед към града?
(*Ee-mah lee stah-yah s eez-gled kuhm grah-dah?*)

268. Is breakfast included in the room rate?
Включена ли е закуската в цената на стаята?
(*Vkloo-cheh-nah lee eh zah-koos-kah-tah v tseh-nah-tah nah stah-yah-tah?*)

269. Can I request a room on a higher floor?
Мога ли да поискам стая на по-висок етаж?
(*Moh-gah lee dah poh-ees-kahm stah-yah nah poh-vee-sohk eh-tahzh?*)

270. Is there an option for a smoking room?
Има ли възможност за стая за пушачи?
(*Ee-mah lee vuhz-mohzh-nost zah stah-yah zah poo-shah-chee?*)

> **Travel Story:** In the Valley of Roses, a rose picker said, "Розите разказват истории" (Roses tell stories), alluding to the deep-rooted tradition of rose oil production.

271. Are there connecting rooms for families?
Има ли свързани стаи за семейства?
(*Ee-mah lee svur-zah-nee stah-ee zah seh-mee-eh-stvah?*)

272. I'd prefer a king-size bed.
Предпочитам легло с размер "кинг-сайз".
(*Prehd-poh-chee-tahm lehg-loh s rahz-mehr "keeng-sighz".*)

273. Is there a bathtub in any of the rooms?
Има ли вана в някоя от стаите?
(*Ee-mah lee vah-nah v nyah-koh-yah oht stah-ee-teh?*)

Hotel Facilities and Services

274. What time does the hotel restaurant close?
До колко часа работи ресторантът на хотела?
(*Doh kohl-koh chah-sah rah-boh-tee reh-stoh-ran-tuht nah hoh-teh-lah?*)

275. Is there a fitness center in the hotel?
Има ли фитнес център в хотела?
(*Ee-mah lee feet-nes tsehn-tur v hoh-teh-lah?*)

276. Can I access the pool as a guest?
Мога ли като гост да ползвам басейна?
(*Moh-gah lee kah-toh gohst dah pohlz-vahm bah-sey-nah?*)

277. Do you offer laundry facilities?
Предлагате ли услуги за пране?
(*Preh-dlah-gah-teh lee oos-loo-ghee zah prah-neh?*)

278. Is parking available on-site?
      Има ли паркинг на мястото на хотела?
      (*Ee-mah lee pahr-keeng nah myahs-toh-toh nah hoh-teh-lah?*)

279. Is room cleaning provided daily?
      Предоставя ли се ежедневно почистване на стаите?
      (*Preh-doh-stah-vyah lee seh eh-zheh-dehv-noh poh-chees-tvah-neh nah stah-ee-teh?*)

280. Can I use the business center?
      Мога ли да използвам бизнес центъра?
      (*Moh-gah lee dah eez-pohlz-vahm beez-nes tsehn-tur-ah?*)

281. Are pets allowed in the hotel?
      Допускат ли се домашни любимци в хотела?
      (*Doh-poo-skaht lee seh doh-mahsh-nee lyoo-beem-tsee v hoh-teh-lah?*)

> **Travel Story:** At a pottery workshop in Troyan, the artisan remarked, "Глината пази ръцете на майстора" (The clay keeps the hands of the master), signifying the artistry in Bulgarian crafts.

Payment and Check-Out

282. Can I have the bill, please?
      Може ли да ми дадете сметката, моля?
      (*Moh-zheh lee dah mee dah-deh-teh smeh-tkah-tah, moh-lyah?*)

283. Do you accept credit cards?
      Приемате ли кредитни карти?
      (*Pree-eh-mah-teh lee kreh-diht-nee kar-tee?*)

284. Can I pay in cash?
Мога ли да платя в брой?
(*Moh-gah lee dah plaht-yah v broy?*)

285. Is there a security deposit required?
Изисква ли се депозит за сигурност?
(*Ee-zeesk-vah lee seh deh-poh-zeet zah see-goor-nost?*)

286. Can I get a receipt for my stay?
Мога ли да получа касова бележка за престоя ми?
(*Moh-gah lee dah poh-loo-chah kah-soh-vah beh-lezh-kah zah preh-sto-yah mee?*)

287. What's the check-out time?
Кога е времето за напускане?
(*Koh-gah eh vreh-meh-toh zah nah-poos-kah-neh?*)

288. Is late check-out an option?
Възможно ли е късно напускане?
(*Vuhz-mohzh-noh lee eh kuh-snoh nah-poos-kah-neh?*)

289. Can I settle my bill in advance?
Мога ли да заплатя сметката предварително?
(*Moh-gah lee dah zah-plah-tyah smeh-tkah-tah prehd-vah-ree-te hl-noh?*)

Booking Accommodations

290. I'd like to make a reservation.
Искам да направя резервация.
(*Ees-kahm dah nah-prah-vyah reh-zer-vah-tsee-yah.*)

70

291. How much is the room rate per night?
Колко струва стаята за нощ?
(*Kohl-koh stroo-vah stah-yah-tah zah nosht?*)

292. Can I book online or by phone?
Мога ли да резервирам онлайн или по телефон?
(*Moh-gah lee dah reh-zer-vee-rahm on-line eely poh teh-leh-fon?*)

293. Are there any special promotions?
Има ли специални промоции?
(*Ee-mah lee speh-tsyahl-nee proh-moh-tsee-eh?*)

294. Is breakfast included in the booking?
Включена ли е закуската в резервацията?
(*Vkloo-cheh-nah lee eh zah-koos-kah-tah v reh-zer-vah-tsee-yah-tah?*)

295. Can you confirm my reservation?
Можете ли да потвърдите моята резервация?
(*Moh-zheh-teh lee dah poh-tvur-dee-teh moh-yah-tah reh-zer-vah-tsee-yah?*)

296. What's the cancellation policy?
Какви са условията за анулиране?
(*Kahk-vee sah oos-loh-vee-yah-tah zah ah-noo-lee-rah-neh?*)

297. I'd like to modify my booking.
Искам да променя резервацията си.
(*Ees-kahm dah proh-mehn-yah reh-zer-vah-tsee-yah-tah see.*)

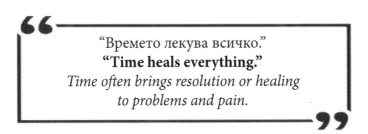

"Времето лекува всичко."
"Time heals everything."
*Time often brings resolution or healing
to problems and pain.*

Mini Lesson:
Basic Grammar Principles in Bulgarian #1

Introduction:

Bulgarian, a South Slavic language, is the official language of Bulgaria. It stands out among Slavic languages for its absence of noun case declension and its use of certain grammatical peculiarities like the evidential verb forms. This lesson provides an introduction to some fundamental concepts of Bulgarian grammar, ideal for those beginning their journey in learning this unique language.

1. The Cyrillic Alphabet:

Bulgarian uses the Cyrillic alphabet, which consists of 30 letters. Each letter corresponds to a specific sound, making the language largely phonetic in nature. For instance, 'Б' is pronounced as 'b', and 'Г' as 'g'.

2. Nouns and Articles:

Unlike most Slavic languages, Bulgarian does not use noun cases. Instead, it has a definite and indefinite article. The definite article is suffixed to the noun, and the indefinite article is implied.

- *Indefinite (no article in English): книга (kniga) - a book*
- *Definite: книгата (knigata) - the book*

3. No Infinitive Form:

Bulgarian verbs do not have an infinitive form. To express purpose or intention, Bulgarian uses a construction with 'да' + the present tense form of the verb. For example:

- *Искам да говоря (Iskam da govorya) - I want to speak*

4. Verb Conjugation:

Bulgarian verbs are conjugated in different tenses, aspects, and moods. They are also conjugated according to person and number in both the past and the present tense. For example:

- *Present tense, 1st person singular: говоря (govorya) - I speak*

5. Evidentiality:

A unique feature of Bulgarian is the use of evidentiality. It is a grammatical category that indicates the source of information. For example:

- *Past aorist tense: видях (vidyah) - I saw (indicating direct knowledge)*

6. Question Formation:

Questions can be formed without rearranging the word order, simply by changing the intonation or by using question words such as 'как?' (how?), 'кога?' (when?), 'къде?' (where?), and 'защо?' (why?).

7. Adjectives:

Adjectives agree with the gender, number, and definiteness of the nouns:

- *Малък град (malak grad) - a small town*
- *Малкият град (malkiyat grad) - the small town*

8. Pronouns:

Bulgarian has personal pronouns, with reflexive pronouns also being used:

- *Аз (Az) - I*
- *Ти (Ti) - You*
- *Себе си (Sebe si) - Myself*

Conclusion:

These fundamental elements of Bulgarian grammar form the foundation for further study. As you delve deeper, you will encounter more complex structures and expressions. Consistent practice and exposure are essential for mastering this intriguing language. Успех! (Good luck!)

SHOPPING

- BARGAINING AND HAGGLING -
- DESCRIBING ITEMS AND SIZES -
- MAKING PURCHASES AND PAYMENTS -

Bargaining

298. Can you give me a discount?
Можете ли да ми направите отстъпка?
(*Moh-zheh-teh lee dah mee nah-prah-vee-teh ot-stup-kah?*)

299. What's your best price?
Каква е вашата най-добра цена?
(*Kahk-vah eh vah-shah-tah nigh-doh-brah tseh-nah?*)

300. Is this the final price?
Това ли е окончателната цена?
(*Toh-vah lee eh oh-kohn-cha-tehl-nah-tah tseh-nah?*)

301. What's the lowest you can go?
Каква е най-ниската цена, на която може да спуснете?
(*Kahk-vah eh nigh-nees-kah-tah tseh-nah, nah koh-yah-toh moh-zheh dah spoos-neh-teh?*)

302. Can you do any better on the price?
Можете ли да предложите по-добра цена?
(*Moh-zheh-teh lee dah preh-dloh-zhee-teh poh-doh-brah tseh-nah?*)

303. Are there any promotions or deals?
Има ли някакви промоции или отстъпки?
(*Ee-mah lee nyah-kah-kvee proh-moh-tsee-eh eely ot-stup-kee?*)

304. I'm on a budget. Can you lower the price?
С ограничен бюджет съм. Можете ли да намалите цената?
(*S oh-grah-nee-chen byoo-jet soom. Moh-zheh-teh lee dah nah-mah-lee-teh tseh-nah-tah?*)

305. I'd like to negotiate the price.
Искам да преговарям за цената.
(*Ees-kahm dah preh-goh-vah-ryahm zah tseh-nah-tah.*)

306. Do you offer any discounts for cash payments?
Предлагате ли отстъпки за плащане в брой?
(*Preh-dlah-gah-teh lee ot-stup-kee zah plahsh-tah-neh v broy?*)

307. Can you match the price from your competitor?
Можете ли да съизмерите цената с тази на конкурента си?
(*Moh-zheh-teh lee dah suh-ees-meh-ree-teh tseh-nah-tah s tah-zee nah kohn-koo-ren-tah see?*)

Item Descriptions

308. Can you tell me about this product?
Можете ли да ми разкажете за този продукт?
(*Moh-zheh-teh lee dah mee rahz-kah-zheh-teh zah toh-zee proh-dookt?*)

309. What are the specifications of this item?
Какви са спецификациите на този артикул?
(*Kahk-vee sah speh-tsee-fee-kah-tsee-ee-teh nah toh-zee ar-tee-kool?*)

310. Is this available in different colors?
Има ли това в различни цветове?
(*Ee-mah lee toh-vah v rahz-leechni tseh-toh-veh?*)

311. Can you explain how this works?
Можете ли да обясните как работи това?
(*Moh-zheh-teh lee dah ob-yah-snee-teh kahk rah-boh-tee toh-vah?*)

312. What's the material of this item?
От какъв материал е направен този продукт?
(*Oht kah-kuv mah-teh-ree-al eh nah-prah-vehn toh-zee proh-dookt?*)

313. Are there any warranties or guarantees?
Има ли гаранции или гаранция за този продукт?
(*Ee-mah lee gah-ran-tsee eely gah-ran-tsee-yah zah toh-zee proh-dookt?*)

314. Does it come with accessories?
Предлага ли се с аксесоари?
(*Preh-dlah-gah lee seh s ahk-seh-so-ah-ree?*)

315. Can you show me how to use this?
Можете ли да ми покажете как се използва това?
(*Moh-zheh-teh lee dah mee poh-kah-zheh-teh kahk seh eez-pohlz-vah toh-vah?*)

316. Are there any size options available?
Има ли различни размери?
(*Ee-mah lee rahz-leechni rahz-meh-ree?*)

317. Can you describe the features of this product?
Можете ли да опишете характеристиките на този продукт?
(*Moh-zheh-teh lee dah oh-pee-sheh-teh hah-rahk-teh-ree-stee-kee-teh nah toh-zee proh-dookt?*)

Payments

318. I'd like to pay with a credit card.
Искам да платя с кредитна карта.
(*Ees-kahm dah plaht-yah s kreh-diht-nah kar-tah.*)

319. Do you accept debit cards?
      Приемате ли дебитни карти?
      (*Pree-eh-mah-teh lee deh-beet-nee kar-tee?*)

320. Can I pay in cash?
      Мога ли да платя в брой?
      (*Moh-gah lee dah plaht-yah v broy?*)

> **Idiomatic Expression:** "Хвърлям око." -
> Meaning: "To take a quick look."
> (Literal translation: "To throw an eye.")

321. What's your preferred payment method?
      Какъв е предпочитаният от вас начин на плащане?
      (*Kah-kuv eh prehd-poh-chee-tah-nee-yat oht vahs nah-cheen nah
      plah-sh-tah-neh?*)

322. Is there an extra charge for using a card?
      Има ли допълнителни такси за ползване на карта?
      (*Ee-mah lee doh-puhl-nee-tehl-nee tahk-see zah pohlz-vah-neh
      nah kar-tah?*)

323. Can I split the payment into installments?
      Мога ли да разсроча плащането на вноски?
      (*Moh-gah lee dah rahz-sroh-chah plahsh-tah-neh-toh nah
      vnoh-skee?*)

324. Do you offer online payment options?
      Предлагате ли опции за онлайн плащане?
      (*Preh-dlah-gah-teh lee op-tsee zah on-line plahsh-tah-neh?*)

325. Can I get a receipt for this purchase?
      Мога ли да получа касова бележка за тази покупка?
      (*Moh-gah lee dah poh-loo-chah kah-soh-vah beh-lezh-kah zah
      tah-zee poh-koo-pkah?*)

326. Are there any additional fees?
Има ли допълнителни такси?
(*Ee-mah lee doh-puhl-nee-tehl-nee tahk-see?*)

327. Is there a minimum purchase amount for card payments?
Има ли минимална сума за плащания с карта?
(*Ee-mah lee mee-nee-mahl-nah soo-mah zah plahsh-tah-nee-yah s kar-tah?*)

> **Travel Story:** During a folklore show in Sofia, a musician stated, "Музиката е езикът на душата" (Music is the language of the soul), expressing the deep connection Bulgarians have with their music.

Asking for Recommendations

328. Can you recommend something popular?
Можете ли да препоръчате нещо популярно?
(*Moh-zheh-teh lee dah preh-poh-roo-chah-teh neh-shtoh poh-poo-lyar-noh?*)

329. What's your best-selling product?
Какъв е вашият най-продаван продукт?
(*Kah-kuv eh vah-shee-yat nigh-proh-dah-vahn proh-dookt?*)

330. Do you have any customer favorites?
Имате ли някои предпочитани продукти от клиентите?
(*Ee-mah-teh lee nyah-koy prehd-poh-chee-tah-nee proh-dook-tee oht klee-ehn-tee-teh?*)

331. Is there a brand you would suggest?
Препоръчвате ли някоя марка?
(*Preh-poh-roo-chvah-teh lee nyah-koh-yah mahr-kah?*)

332. Could you point me to high-quality items?

Можете ли да ми покажете продукти от високо качество?

(Moh-zheh-teh lee dah mee poh-kah-zheh-teh proh-dook-tee oht vee-soh-koh kah-ches-tvoh?)

333. What do most people choose in this category?

Какво обикновено избират хората в тази категория?

(Kahk-voh oh-beek-noh-veh-noh eez-bee-raht hoh-rah-tah v tah-zee kah-teh-goh-ree-yah?)

334. Are there any special recommendations?

Имате ли специални препоръки?

(Ee-mah-teh lee speh-tsyahl-nee preh-poh-roo-kee?)

335. Can you tell me what's trendy right now?

Можете ли да ми кажете какво е модерно в момента?

(Moh-zheh-teh lee dah mee kah-zheh-teh kahk-voh eh moh-dehr-noh v moh-mehn-tah?)

336. What's your personal favorite here?

Какво е вашето лично предпочитание тук?

(Kahk-voh eh vah-sheh-toh lee-chnoh prehd-poh-chee-tah-nee-eh took?)

337. Any suggestions for a gift?

Имате ли предложения за подарък?

(Ee-mah-teh lee prehd-loh-zheh-nee-yah zah poh-dah-ruk?)

Language Learning Tip: Watch Bulgarian TV Shows - They are great for casual language and culture.

Returns and Exchanges

338.   I'd like to return this item.
Искам да върна този продукт.
(*Ees-kahm dah vuhr-nah toh-zee proh-dookt.*)

339.   Can I exchange this for a different size?
Мога ли да заменя това с друг размер?
(*Moh-gah lee dah zah-mehn-yah toh-vah s droog rahz-mehr?*)

340.   What's your return policy?
Каква е вашата политика за връщане?
(*Kahk-vah eh vah-shah-tah poh-lee-tee-kah zah vruhsh-tah-neh?*)

341.   Is there a time limit for returns?
Има ли времеви лимит за връщане?
(*Ee-mah lee vreh-meh-vee lee-miht zah vruhsh-tah-neh?*)

342.   Do I need a receipt for a return?
Нужна ли е касова бележка за връщане?
(*Noozh-nah lee eh kah-soh-vah beh-lezh-kah zah vruhsh-tah-neh?*)

343.   Is there a restocking fee for returns?
Има ли такса за презареждане при връщане?
(*Ee-mah lee tahk-sah zah preh-zah-rezh-dah-neh pree vruhsh-tah-neh?*)

344.   Can I get a refund or store credit?
Мога ли да получа възстановяване на сумата или кредит в магазина?
(*Moh-gah lee dah poh-loo-chah vuhs-toh-noh-vyah-vah-neh nah soo-mah-tah eely kreh-diht v mah-gah-zee-nah?*)

345. Do you offer exchanges without receipts?
Предлагате ли замяна без касова бележка?
(*Preh-dlah-gah-teh lee zah-myah-nah behz kah-soh-vah beh-lezh-kah?*)

346. What's the process for returning a defective item?
Какъв е процесът за връщане на дефектен продукт?
(*Kah-kuv eh proh-tseh-suht zah vruhsh-tah-neh nah deh-fek-tehn proh-dookt?*)

347. Can I return an online purchase in-store?
Мога ли да върна онлайн покупка в магазина?
(*Moh-gah lee dah vuhr-nah on-line poh-koo-pkah v mah-gah-zee-nah?*)

> **Travel Story:** At a vineyard in the Thracian Valley, a winemaker toasted, "Всяко вино разказва история" (Every wine tells a story), highlighting the rich tradition of Bulgarian winemaking.

Shopping for Souvenirs

348. I'm looking for local souvenirs.
Търся местни сувенири.
(*Tur-syah mehs-tee soo-veh-nee-ree.*)

349. What's a popular souvenir from this place?
Какъв е популярен сувенир от това място?
(*Kah-kuv eh poh-poo-lyah-ren soo-veh-neer oht toh-vah myahs-toh?*)

350. Do you have any handmade souvenirs?
Имате ли ръчно изработени сувенири?
(*Ee-mah-teh lee ruhch-noh eez-rah-boh-teh-nee soo-veh-nee-ree?*)

351. Are there any traditional items here?
Има ли тук традиционни предмети?
(*Ee-mah lee took trah-dee-tsee-on-nee prehd-meh-tee?*)

352. Can you suggest a unique souvenir?
Можете ли да предложите уникален сувенир?
(*Moh-zheh-teh lee dah prehd-loh-zhee-teh oo-nee-kah-len soo-veh-neer?*)

353. I want something that represents this city.
Искам нещо, което представлява този град.
(*Ees-kahm neh-shtoh, koh-eh-toh prehd-stahv-lyah-vah toh-zee grahd.*)

354. Are there souvenirs for a specific landmark?
Има ли сувенири за конкретна забележителност?
(*Ee-mah lee soo-veh-nee-ree zah kohn-kreh-tah zah-beh-leh-zhee-tehl-nohst?*)

355. Can you show me souvenirs with cultural significance?
Можете ли да ми покажете сувенири с културно значение?
(*Moh-zheh-teh lee dah mee poh-kah-zheh-teh soo-veh-nee-ree s kool-toor-noh znah-cheh-nyeh?*)

356. Do you offer personalized souvenirs?
Предлагате ли персонализирани сувенири?
(*Preh-dlah-gah-teh lee pehr-soh-nah-lee-zee-rah-nee soo-veh-nee-ree?*)

357. What's the price range for souvenirs?
Какъв е ценовият диапазон за сувенири?
(*Kah-kuv eh tseh-noh-vee-yat dee-ah-pah-zohn zah soo-veh-nee-ree?*)

Shopping Online

358. How do I place an order online?
Как да направя поръчка онлайн?
(*Kahk dah nah-prah-vyah poh-ruhch-kah on-line?*)

359. What's the website for online shopping?
Какъв е уебсайтът за онлайн пазаруване?
(*Kah-kuv eh ueb-sigh-tuht zah on-line pah-zah-roo-vah-neh?*)

360. Do you offer free shipping?
Предлагате ли безплатна доставка?
(*Preh-dlah-gah-teh lee behz-plaht-nah doh-stahv-kah?*)

361. Are there any online discounts or promotions?
Има ли онлайн отстъпки или промоции?
(*Ee-mah lee on-line ot-stup-kee eely proh-moh-tsee-eh?*)

362. Can I track my online order?
Мога ли да проследя онлайн поръчката си?
(*Moh-gah lee dah proh-sleh-dyah on-line poh-ruhch-kah-tah see?*)

363. What's the return policy for online purchases?
Каква е политиката за връщане на онлайн покупки?
(*Kahk-vah eh poh-lee-tee-kah-tah zah vruhsh-tah-neh nah on-line poh-koo-pkee?*)

364. Do you accept various payment methods online?
Приемате ли различни онлайн платежни методи?
(*Pree-eh-mah-teh lee rahz-leechni on-line pla-tezh-nee meh-toh-dee?*)

365. Is there a customer support hotline for online orders?
Има ли гореща линия за поддръжка на клиенти за онлайн поръчки?
(*Ee-mah lee goh-resht-ah lee-nee-yah zah pod-druhzh-kah nah klee-en-tee zah on-line poh-ruhch-kee?*)

> **Idiomatic Expression:** "Да ти е сладко." - Meaning: "Enjoy it, often used sarcastically." (Literal translation: "May it be sweet to you.")

366. Can I change or cancel my online order?
Мога ли да променя или анулирам моята онлайн поръчка?
(*Moh-gah lee dah proh-mehn-yah eely ah-noo-lee-rahm moh-yah-tah on-line poh-ruhch-kah?*)

367. What's the delivery time for online purchases?
Колко време отнема доставката за онлайн покупки?
(*Kohl-koh vreh-meh oht-neh-mah doh-stahv-kah-tah zah on-line poh-koo-pkee?*)

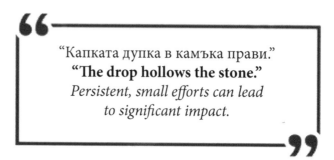

"Капката дупка в камъка прави."
"The drop hollows the stone."
Persistent, small efforts can lead to significant impact.

Cross Word Puzzle: Shopping

(Provide the English translation for the following Bulgarian words)

Down

1. - ЦЕНА
3. - ПОРТФЕЙЛ
4. - МАРКА
5. - КАСОВА БЕЛЕЖКА
8. - ОТСТЪПКА
9. - КЛИЕНТ
11. - ПАЗАРУВАНЕ

Across

2. - КОЛИЧКА
5. - ТЪРГОВИЯ НА ДРЕБНО
6. - РАЗПРОДАЖБА
7. - ГИЩЕ
9. - ДРЕХИ
10. - БУТИК
12. - КАСИЕР

Correct Answers:

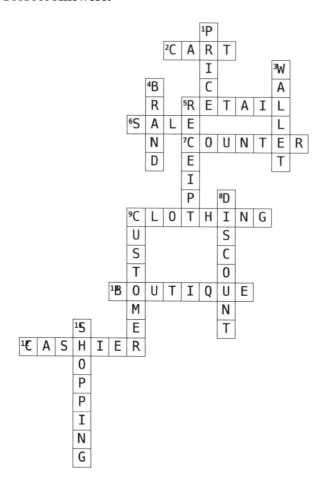

EMERGENCIES

- SEEKING HELP IN CASE OF AN EMERGENCY -
- REPORTING ACCIDENTS OR HEALTH ISSUES -
- CONTACTING AUTHORITIES OR MEDICAL SERVICES -

Getting Help in Emergencies

368.   Call an ambulance, please.
        Моля, повикайте линейка.
        (Moh-lyah, poh-vee-kigh-teh lee-ney-kah.)

> **Language Learning Tip:** Immerse Yourself - Surround yourself with the Bulgarian language.

369.   I need a doctor right away.
        Нужен ми е лекар веднага.
        (Noo-zhen mee eh leh-kar vehd-nah-gah.)

370.   Is there a hospital nearby?
        Има ли болница наблизо?
        (Ee-mah lee bohl-nee-tsah nah-blee-zoh?)

371.   Help! I've lost my way.
        Помощ! Изгубих се.
        (Poh-mosht! Eez-goo-beeh seh.)

372.   Can you call the police?
        Можете ли да извикате полицията?
        (Moh-zheh-teh lee dah eez-vee-kah-teh poh-lee-tsyah-tah?)

373.   Someone, please call for help.
        Някой, моля, повикайте за помощ.
        (Nyah-koy, moh-lyah, poh-vee-kigh-teh zah poh-mosht.)

374.   My friend is hurt, we need assistance.
        Моят приятел е ранен, нуждаем се от помощ.
        (Moh-yaht pree-ya-tel eh rah-nen, noozh-day-em seh oht poh-mosht.)

375. I've been robbed; I need the authorities.
Обран съм; нуждая се от властите.
(*Oh-brahn sum; noozh-dah-yah seh oht vlah-stee-teh.*)

376. Please, I need immediate assistance.
Моля, нуждая се от незабавна помощ.
(*Moh-lyah, noozh-dah-yah seh oht neh-zah-bahv-nah poh-mosht.*)

377. Is there a fire station nearby?
Има ли пожарна близо?
(*Ee-mah lee poh-zhahr-nah bleeh-zoh?*)

Reporting Incidents

378. I've witnessed an accident.
Станах свидетел на инцидент.
(*Stah-nahkh svee-deh-tel nah een-tsee-dehnt.*)

379. There's been a car crash.
Стана катастрофа с кола.
(*Stah-nah kah-tah-stroh-fah s koh-lah.*)

380. We need to report a fire.
Трябва да съобщим за пожар.
(*Tryahb-vah dah suh-ohb-sheem zah poh-zhar.*)

381. Someone has stolen my wallet.
Някой ми открадна портфейла.
(*Nyah-koy mee oht-krahd-nah pohrt-fey-lah.*)

382. I need to report a lost passport.
Трябва да съобщя за изгубен паспорт.
(*Tryahb-vah dah suh-ohb-shyah zah eez-goo-ben pahs-port.*)

383. There's a suspicious person here.
Тук има подозрителен човек.
(*Took ee-mah poh-doh-zree-teh-len choh-vek.*)

384. I've found a lost child.
Намерих изгубено дете.
(*Nah-meh-reeh eez-goo-beh-noh deh-teh.*)

385. Can you help me report a missing person?
Можете ли да ми помогнете да съобщя за изчезнало лице?
(*Moh-zheh-teh lee dah mee poh-moh-gneh-teh dah suh-ohb-shyah zah eez-chehz-nah-loh lee-tseh?*)

386. We've had a break-in at our home.
Имаше взлом в нашия дом.
(*Ee-mah-sheh vz-lom v nah-shee-yah dohm.*)

387. I need to report a damaged vehicle.
Трябва да съобщя за повредено превозно средство.
(*Tryahb-vah dah suh-ohb-shyah zah poh-vreh-deh-noh preh-vohz-noh srehd-stvoh.*)

Contacting Authorities

388. I'd like to speak to the police.
Искам да говоря с полицията.
(*Ees-kahm dah goh-voh-ryah s poh-lee-tsyah-tah.*)

389. I need to contact the embassy.
Трябва да се свържа с посолството.
(*Tryahb-vah dah seh svuhr-zhah s poh-sohl-stvoh-toh.*)

390. Can you connect me to the fire department?
Можете ли да ме свържете с пожарната?
(*Moh-zheh-teh lee dah meh svuhr-zheh-teh s poh-zhar-nah-tah?*)

391. We need to reach animal control.
Трябва да се свържем със службата за животни.
(*Tryahb-vah dah seh svuhr-zhem suhs sloozh-bah-tah zah zhi-vot-nee.*)

392. How do I get in touch with the coast guard?
Как да се свържа с бреговата охрана?
(*Kahk dah seh svuhr-zhah s breh-goh-vah-tah oh-hrah-nah?*)

393. I'd like to report a noise complaint.
Искам да подам жалба за шум.
(*Ees-kahm dah poh-dahm zhahl-bah zah shoom.*)

394. I need to contact child protective services.
Трябва да се свържа със службата за защита на децата.
(*Tryahb-vah dah seh svuhr-zhah suhs sloozh-bah-tah zah zahshtee-tah nah deh-tsah-tah.*)

395. Is there a hotline for disaster relief?
Има ли телефон за спешна помощ при бедствия?
(*Ee-mah lee teh-leh-fohn zah spehsh-nah poh-mosht pree behd-stvee-yah?*)

> **Fun Fact:** Bulgaria has a long history of wine production and is one of the world's largest wine producers.

396. I want to report a hazardous situation.
Искам да съобщя за опасна ситуация.
(*Ees-kahm dah suh-ohb-shyah zah oh-pahs-nah see-too-ah-tsee-yah.*)

397. I need to reach the environmental agency.
Трябва да се свържа с агенцията за околната среда.
(*Tryahb-vah dah seh svuhr-zhah s ah-gen-tsyah-tah zah oh-kohl-nah-tah sreh-dah.*)

> **Travel Story:** In the charming streets of Nesebar, a local historian commented, "Всеки камък тук има своя история" (Every stone here has its story), reflecting on the ancient city's rich past.

Medical Emergencies

398. I'm feeling very ill.
Чувствам се много зле.
(*Choo-vst-vahm seh mnoh-goh zleh.*)

399. There's been an accident; we need a medic.
Стана инцидент; нуждаем се от лекар.
(*Stah-nah een-tsee-dehnt; noozh-day-em seh oht leh-kahr.*)

400. Call 112; it's a medical emergency.
Обадете се на 112; става въпрос за медицинска спешност.
(*Oh-bah-deh-teh seh nah sto edin dva; stah-vah vu-p-rohs zah meh-dee-tseen-skah spehsh-nohst.*)

> **Fun Fact:** Mount Musala is the highest peak in the Balkan Peninsula.

401. We need an ambulance right away.
Трябва ни линейка веднага.
(*Tryahb-vah nee lee-ney-kah vehd-nah-gah.*)

402. I'm having trouble breathing.
Имам проблеми с дишането.
(*Ee-mahm proh-bleh-mee s dee-shah-neh-toh.*)

403. Someone has lost consciousness.
Някой загуби съзнание.
(*Nyah-koy zah-goo-bee suhz-nah-nee-eh.*)

404. I think it's a heart attack; call for help.
Мисля, че е инфаркт; повикайте за помощ.
(*Mees-lyah, cheh eh een-fahrkt; poh-vee-kigh-teh zah poh-mosht.*)

405. There's been a severe injury.
Имаше сериозно нараняване.
(*Ee-mah-sheh seh-ree-ohz-noh nah-rahn-yah-vah-neh.*)

406. I need immediate medical attention.
Нуждая се от незабавна медицинска помощ.
(*Noozh-dah-yah seh oht neh-zah-bahv-nah meh-dee-tseen-skah poh-mosht.*)

407. Is there a first-aid station nearby?
Има ли пункт за първа помощ наблизо?
(*Ee-mah lee poonkt zah pur-vah poh-mosht nah-blee-zoh?*)

> **Idiomatic Expression:** "Хващам се на бас." -
> Meaning: "To bet on something."
> (Literal translation: "I catch myself on a bet.")

Fire and Safety

408. There's a fire; call 112!
      Има пожар; обадете се на 112!
      (*Ee-mah poh-zhar; oh-bah-deh-teh seh nah sto edin dva!*)

409. We need to evacuate the building.
      Трябва да евакуираме сградата.
      (*Tryahb-vah dah eh-vah-koo-ee-rah-meh sgrah-dah-tah.*)

410. Fire extinguisher, quick!
      Пожарогасител, бързо!
      (*Poh-zhah-roh-gah-see-tehl, buhr-zoh!*)

411. I smell gas; we need to leave.
      Усещам газ; трябва да тръгнем.
      (*Oo-seh-shahm gahz; tryahb-vah dah truhg-nem.*)

> **Fun Fact:** Bulgaria has a rich Thracian heritage, with numerous ancient tombs and artifacts.

412. Can you contact the fire department?
      Можете ли да се обадите в пожарната?
      (*Moh-zheh-teh lee dah seh oh-bah-dee-teh v poh-zhar-nah-tah?*)

413. There's a hazardous spill; we need help.
      Има опасно разливане; нуждаем се от помощ.
      (*Ee-mah oh-pahs-noh rahz-lee-vah-neh; noozh-day-em seh oht poh-mosht.*)

414. Is there a fire escape route?
      Има ли път за бягство при пожар?
      (*Ee-mah lee puht zah byahg-stvoh pree poh-zhar?*)

415. This area is not safe; we need to move.
Тази област не е безопасна; трябва да се местим.
(*Tah-zee ob-lahst neh eh behz-oh-pahs-nah; tryahb-vah dah seh mehs-teem.*)

416. Alert, there's a potential explosion.
Внимание, има опасност от взрив.
(*Vnee-mah-nee-eh, ee-mah oh-pahs-nost oht vzreev.*)

417. I see smoke; we need assistance.
Виждам дим; нуждаем се от помощ.
(*Veezh-dahm deem; noozh-day-em seh oht poh-mosht.*)

Natural Disasters

418. It's an earthquake; take cover!
Има земетресение; укривайте се!
(*Ee-mah zeh-meh-treh-seh-nee-eh; oo-kree-vigh-teh seh!*)

419. We're experiencing a tornado; find shelter.
Има торнадо; намерете убежище.
(*Ee-mah tor-nah-doh; nah-meh-reh-teh oo-beh-zheesh-teh.*)

420. Flood warning; move to higher ground.
Предупреждение за наводнение; преместете се на по-високо място.
(*Preh-doo-prehzh-deh-nee-eh zah nah-vohd-neh-nee-eh; preh-mehs-teh-teh seh nah poh-vee-soh-koh myahs-toh.*)

421. We need to prepare for a hurricane.
Трябва да се подготвим за ураган.
(*Tryahb-vah dah seh pohd-goh-tveem zah oo-rah-gahn.*)

422. This is a tsunami alert; head inland.
Това е предупреждение за цунами; отидете вътре в страната.
(*Toh-vah eh preh-doo-prezh-deh-nee-eh zah tsoo-nah-mee; oh-tee-deh-teh vuht-reh v strah-nah-tah.*)

> **Fun Fact:** Bulgaria is home to many beautifully preserved monasteries with rich histories.

423. It's a wildfire; evacuate immediately.
Има горски пожар; евакуирайте се незабавно.
(*Ee-mah gor-skee poh-zhar; eh-vah-koo-ee-rah-yteh seh neh-zah-bahv-noh.*)

424. There's a volcanic eruption; take precautions.
Има вулканично изригване; предприемете предпазни мерки.
(*Ee-mah vool-kah-neech-noh eez-reeg-vah-neh; prehd-pree-eh-meh-teh prehd-pahz-nee mehr-kee.*)

425. We've had an avalanche; help needed.
Има лавина; нуждаем се от помощ.
(*Ee-mah lah-vee-nah; noozh-day-em seh oht poh-mosht.*)

426. Earthquake aftershock; stay indoors.
Следват вторични трусове от земетресението; останете вътре.
(*Sleh-dvaht vtoh-reech-nee troo-soh-veh oht zeh-meh-treh-seh-nee-eh-toh; oh-stah-neh-teh vuht-reh.*)

427. Severe thunderstorm; seek shelter.
Силна гръмотевична буря; потърсете убежище.
(*Seel-nah gruh-moh-teh-veech-nah boor-yah; poh-tuhr-seh-teh oo-beh-zheesh-teh.*)

Emergency Services Information

428. What's the emergency hotline number?
Какъв е номерът на спешната линия?
(Kah-kuv eh noh-meh-ruht nah spehsh-nah lee-nee-yah?)

429. Where's the nearest police station?
Къде е най-близкото полицейско управление?
(Kuh-deh eh nie-bleez-koh-toh poh-lee-tsey-skoh oo-prahv-leh-nee-eh?)

430. How do I contact the fire department?
Как да се свържа с пожарната?
(Kahk dah seh s-vuhr-zhah s poh-zhar-nah-tah?)

431. Is there a hospital nearby?
Има ли болница наблизо?
(Ee-mah lee bohl-nee-tsa nah-blee-zoh?)

432. What's the number for poison control?
Какъв е номерът за отравяне?
(Kah-kuv eh noh-meh-ruht zah o-trah-vyah-neh?)

433. Where can I find a disaster relief center?
Къде мога да намеря център за помощ при бедствия?
(Kuh-deh moh-gah dah nah-meh-ryah tsehn-tuhr zah poh-mosht pree behd-stvee-yah?)

> **Fun Fact:** Plovdiv is one of the oldest continuously inhabited cities in Europe.

434. What's the local emergency radio station?
Каква е местната спешна радиостанция?
(*Kah-kvah eh mehs-tah-tah spehsh-nah rah-dee-oh-stahn-tsee-ah?*)

435. Are there any shelters in the area?
Има ли убежища в района?
(*Ee-mah lee oo-beh-zhish-tah v rah-yoh-nah?*)

436. Who do I call for road assistance?
На кого да се обадя за пътна помощ?
(*Nah koh-goh dah seh oh-bahd-yah zah puht-nah poh-mosht?*)

437. How can I reach search and rescue teams?
Как мога да се свържа с екипи за търсене и спасяване?
(*Kahk moh-gah dah seh s-vuhr-zhah s eh-kee-pee zah tuhr-seh-neh ee spah-syah-vah-neh?*)

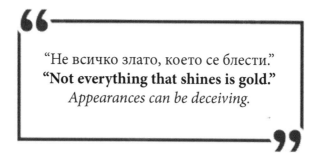

"Не всичко злато, което се блести."
"Not everything that shines is gold."
Appearances can be deceiving.

Interactive Challenge: Emergencies Quiz

1. **How do you say "emergency" in Bulgarian?**

   a) Ябълка
   b) Спешен случай
   c) Сирене
   d) Плаж

2. **What's the Bulgarian word for "ambulance"?**

   a) Кола
   b) Колело
   c) Линейка
   d) Училище

3. **If you need immediate medical attention, what should you say in Bulgarian?**

   a) Искам хляб.
   b) Къде е гарата?
   c) Трябва ми спешна медицинска помощ.

4. **How do you ask "Is there a hospital nearby?" in Bulgarian?**

   a) Къде е киното?
   b) Имате ли химикал?
   c) Има ли болница наблизо?

5. **What's the Bulgarian word for "police"?**

   a) Ябълка
   b) Полиция
   c) Влак

6. **How do you say "fire" in Bulgarian?**

   a) Слънце
   b) Куче
   c) Огън
   d) Книга

7. **If you've witnessed an accident, what phrase can you use in Bulgarian?**

   a) Искам шоколад.
   b) Видях катастрофа.
   c) Харесвам цветята.
   d) Това е моят дом.

8. **What's the Bulgarian word for "help"?**

   a) Довиждане
   b) Добър ден
   c) Благодаря
   d) Помощ!

9. **How would you say "I've been robbed; I need the authorities" in Bulgarian?**

   a) Ядох сирене.
   b) Ограбен съм; нуждая се от властите.
   c) Това е красива планина.

10. **How do you ask "Can you call an ambulance, please?" in Bulgarian?**

    a) Можете ли да повикате такси, моля?
    b) Можете ли да ми дадете сол?
    c) Можете ли да повикате линейка, моля?

11. What's the Bulgarian word for "emergency services"?

a) Спешни услуги
b) Вкусна торта
c) Лек

12. How do you say "reporting an accident" in Bulgarian?

a) Да пея песен
b) Да чета книга
c) Да докладвам за катастрофа

13. If you need to contact the fire department, what should you say in Bulgarian?

a) Как да стигна до библиотеката?
b) Трябва да се свържа с пожарната.
c) Търся приятеля си.

14. What's the Bulgarian word for "urgent"?

a) Малък
b) Красив
c) Бърз
d) Спешен

15. How do you ask for the nearest police station in Bulgarian?

a) Къде е най-близката пекарна?
b) Къде е най-близкото полицейско управление?
c) Имате ли карта?
d) Колко е часът?

Correct Answers:

1. b)
2. c)
3. c)
4. c)
5. b)
6. c)
7. b)
8. d)
9. b)
10. c)
11. a)
12. c)
13. b)
14. d)
15. b)

EVERYDAY CONVERSATIONS

- SMALL TALK AND CASUAL CONVERSATIONS -
- DISCUSSING THE WEATHER, HOBBIES, AND INTERESTS -
- MAKING PLANS WITH FRIENDS OR ACQUAINTANCES -

Small Talk

438. How's it going?
Как върви?
(*Kahk vuhr-vi?*)

439. Nice weather we're having, isn't it?
Хубаво време, нали?
(*Hoo-bah-voh vreh-meh, nah-lee?*)

440. Have any exciting plans for the weekend?
Имате ли интересни планове за уикенда?
(*Ee-mah-teh lee een-teh-res-nee plah-no-veh zah oo-ee-ken-dah?*)

441. Did you catch that new movie?
Гледахте ли новия филм?
(*Gleh-dahkh-teh lee noh-vee-yah feelm?*)

442. How's your day been so far?
Как е минал денят ви досега?
(*Kahk eh mee-nahl deh-nyat vee doh-seh-gah?*)

443. What do you do for work?
С какво се занимавате?
(*S kah-kvoh seh zah-nee-mah-vah-teh?*)

444. Do you come here often?
Често ли идвате тук?
(*Chehs-toh lee eed-vah-teh took?*)

445. Have you tried the food at this place before?
Пробвали ли сте храната тук преди?
(*Proh-bvah-lee lee steh khra-nah-tah took preh-dee?*)

446. Any recommendations for things to do in town?
Имате ли препоръки за неща за правене в града?
(*Ee-mah-teh lee preh-poh-ruh-kee zah neh-shtah zah prah-veh-neh v grah-dah?*)

447. Do you follow any sports teams?
Подкрепяте ли някой спортен отбор?
(*Pod-kreh-pyah-teh lee nyah-koy spohr-ten oht-bohr?*)

448. Have you traveled anywhere interesting lately?
Пътували ли сте наскоро някъде интересно?
(*Puh-too-vah-lee lee steh nah-skoh-roh nyahk-deh een-teh-res-noh?*)

449. Do you enjoy cooking?
Харесва ли ви да готвите?
(*Hah-rehs-vah lee vee dah goht-vee-teh?*)

> **Travel Story:** On the slopes of Bansko, a ski instructor mentioned, "Планината учи" (The mountain teaches), referring to the life lessons learned while skiing.

Casual Conversations

450. What's your favorite type of music?
Какъв е любимият ви музикален жанр?
(*Kah-kuv eh lyoo-bee-mee-yat vee moo-zee-kah-len zhanr?*)

> **Fun Fact:** The Bulgarian Black Sea Coast is famous for its beaches and resorts.

451. How do you like to spend your free time?
Как обичате да прекарвате свободното си време?
(*Kahk oh-bee-cha-teh dah preh-kar-va-teh svoh-bod-noh-toh see vreh-meh?*)

452. Do you have any pets?
Имате ли домашни любимци?
(*Ee-mah-teh lee doh-mahsh-nee lyoo-beem-tsi?*)

453. Where did you grow up?
Къде сте израснали?
(*Kuh-deh steh eez-ras-nah-lee?*)

454. What's your family like?
Какво е семейството ви?
(*Kahk-voh eh seh-my-yes-toh-voh vee?*)

455. Are you a morning person or a night owl?
Сутрешен човек ли сте или нощна птица?
(*Soo-treh-shehn choh-vehk lee steh ee-lee nosht-nah ptee-tsah?*)

456. Do you prefer coffee or tea?
Предпочитате ли кафе или чай?
(*Prehd-poh-chee-tah-teh lee kah-feh ee-lee chai?*)

457. Are you into any TV shows right now?
Гледате ли някое телевизионно предаване в момента?
(*Gleh-dah-teh lee nyah-koh-eh teh-leh-vee-zee-on-noh preh-dah-vah-neh v moh-men-tah?*)

> **Idiomatic Expression:** "Завивам се в мълчание." -
> Meaning: "To keep silent."
> (Literal translation: "To wrap myself in silence.")

458. What's the last book you read?
Коя е последната книга, която сте прочели?
(*Koh-yah eh pohs-lehd-nah-tah klee-gah, koh-yah-toh steh proh-cheh-lee?*)

459. Do you like to travel?
Харесва ли ви да пътувате?
(*Hah-rehs-vah lee vee dah puht-oo-vah-teh?*)

460. Are you a fan of outdoor activities?
Обичате ли активности на открито?
(*Oh-bee-cha-teh lee ak-teev-nohs-tee nah ot-kree-toh?*)

461. How do you unwind after a long day?
Как се отпускате след дълъг ден?
(*Kahk seh ot-poos-kah-teh slehd duh-luhg dehn?*)

Discussing the Weather

462. Can you believe this heat/cold?
Можете ли да повярвате в тази жега/студ?
(*Moh-zheh-teh lee dah poh-vyah-rvah-teh v tah-zee zheh-gah/stood?*)

463. I heard it's going to rain all week.
Чух, че цялата седмица ще вали.
(*Chuh, cheh tsee-yah-lah-tah sehd-mee-tsah shteh vah-lee.*)

464. What's the temperature like today?
Каква е температурата днес?
(*Kahk-vah eh tehm-peh-rah-too-rah-tah dnes?*)

465. Do you like sunny or cloudy days better?
Предпочитате ли слънчеви или облачни дни?
(*Pred-poh-chee-tah-teh lee sluhn-cheh-vee ee-lee ob-lahch-nee dni?*)

466. Have you ever seen a snowstorm like this?
Виждали ли сте някога такава снежна буря?
(*Veezh-dah-lee lee steh nyah-koh-gah tah-kah-vah snezh-nah boo-ryah?*)

467. Is it always this humid here?
Винаги ли е толкова влажно тук?
(*Vee-nah-gee lee eh tol-koh-vah vlahzh-noh took?*)

468. Did you get caught in that thunderstorm yesterday?
Попаднахте ли в тази гръмотевична буря вчера?
(*Poh-pahd-nahh-teh lee v tah-zee gruh-mo-teh-veech-nah boo-ryah vcheh-rah?*)

469. What's the weather like in your hometown?
Какво е времето в родния ви град?
(*Kahk-voh eh vreh-meh-toh v rohd-nee-yah vee grahd?*)

470. I can't stand the wind; how about you?
Не мога да понасям вятъра; а вие?
(*Neh moh-gah dah poh-nah-syahm vyah-tuh-rah; ah vee-eh?*)

471. Is it true the winters here are mild?
Вярно ли е, че зимите тук са меки?
(*Vyahr-noh lee eh, cheh zee-mee-teh took sah meh-kee?*)

472. Do you like beach weather?
Харесва ли ви плажното време?
(*Hah-rehs-vah lee vee plahzh-noh-toh vreh-meh?*)

473. How do you cope with the humidity in summer?
Как се справяте с влажността през лятото?
(*Kahk seh sprah-vyah-teh s vlahzh-nost-tah prehz lyah-toh-toh?*)

Hobbies

474. What are your hobbies or interests?
Какви са вашите хобита или интереси?
(*Kahk-vee sah vah-shee-teh hoh-bee-tah ee-lee een-teh-reh-see?*)

475. Do you play any musical instruments?
Свирите ли на някой музикален инструмент?
(*Svee-ree-teh lee nah nyah-koy moo-zee-kah-len een-stroo-ment?*)

476. Have you ever tried painting or drawing?
Пробвали ли сте някога да рисувате или да рисувате?
(*Prohb-vah-lee lee steh nyah-koh-gah dah ree-soo-vah-teh ee-lee dah ree-soo-vah-teh?*)

477. Are you a fan of sports?
Фен ли сте на спорта?
(*Fehn lee steh nah spohr-tah?*)

478. Do you enjoy cooking or baking?
Харесва ли ви да готвите или да печете?
(*Hah-rehs-vah lee vee dah goht-vee-teh ee-lee dah peh-cheh-teh?*)

479. Are you into photography?
Харесва ли ти фотографията?
(*Ha-rehs-vah lee tee foh-toh-grah-fiyah-tah?*)

480. Have you ever tried gardening?
Пробвал(а) ли си някога градинарство?
(*Prob-val(a) lee see nyah-koh-gah grah-dee-narst-voh?*)

481. Do you like to read in your free time?
Харесва ли ти да четеш в свободното си време?
(*Ha-rehs-vah lee tee dah cheh-tesh v svoh-bod-noh-toh see vreh-meh?*)

482. Have you explored any new hobbies lately?
Разглеждал(а) ли си напоследък нови хобита?
(*Raz-glehzh-dahl(a) lee see nah-poh-sleh-dahk noh-vee hoh-bee-tah?*)

483. Are you a collector of anything?
Колекционер ли си на нещо?
(*Koh-lehk-tsyoh-nehr lee see nah neh-shtoh?*)

484. Do you like to watch movies or TV shows?
Харесва ли ти да гледаш филми или телевизионни предавания?
(*Ha-rehs-vah lee tee dah gleh-dahsh feel-mee ee-lee teh-leh-vi-zee-on-nee preh-dah-vah-nee-yah?*)

485. Have you ever taken up a craft project?
Занимавал(а) ли си се някога с ръкоделие?
(*Zah-nee-mah-vahl(a) lee see seh nyah-koh-gah s ruh-koh-deh-lee-eh?*)

> **Idiomatic Expression:** "Пускам се на течението." -
> Meaning: "To go with the flow."
> (Literal translation: "To let myself to the current.")

Interests

486. What topics are you passionate about?
За кои теми сте страстен?
(Zah koy teh-mee steh strahs-ten?)

487. Are you involved in any social causes?
Ангажиран ли си с социални каузи?
(An-gah-zhee-rahn lee see s soh-tsyahl-nee kow-zee?)

488. Do you enjoy learning new languages?
Харесва ли ти да учиш нови езици?
(Ha-rehs-vah lee tee dah oo-cheesh noh-vee eh-zee-tsee?)

489. Are you into fitness or wellness?
Интересуваш ли се от фитнес или уелнес?
(Een-teh-reh-soo-vahsh lee seh oht feet-nes ee-lee uel-nes?)

490. Are you a technology enthusiast?
Запален ли си по технологиите?
(Zah-pah-lehn lee see poh teh-hnoh-loh-gee-ee-teh?)

491. What's your favorite genre of books or movies?
Какъв е любимият ти жанр на книги или филми?
(Kah-kahv eh lyoo-bee-mee-yat tee zhanr nah k-nee-gee ee-lee feel-mee?)

492. Do you follow current events or politics?
Следваш ли текущите събития или политиката?
(Sleh-dvahsh lee too-chee-teh suh-bee-tee-yah ee-lee poh-lee-tee-kah-tah?)

493.   Are you into fashion or design?
Интересуваш ли се от мода или дизайн?
(*Een-teh-reh-soo-vahsh lee seh oht moh-dah ee-lee dee-zah-een?*)

494.   Are you a history buff?
Интересуваш ли се от история?
(*Een-teh-reh-soo-vahsh lee seh oht ees-toh-ree-yah?*)

495.   Have you ever been involved in volunteer work?
Участвал(а) ли си някога в доброволческа работа?
(*Ooh-chah-stvahl(a) lee see nyah-koh-gah v doh-broh-vohl-chehs-kah rah-boh-tah?*)

496.   Are you passionate about cooking or food culture?
Страстен(а) ли си по готвене или кулинарна култура?
(*Strah-stehn(a) lee see poh goht-veh-neh ee-lee koo-lee-nahr-nah kool-too-rah?*)

497.   Are you an advocate for any specific hobbies or interests?
Предпочиташ ли някои конкретни хобита или интереси?
(*Prehd-poh-chee-tahsh lee nyah-koy kohn-kreh-tee hoh-bee-tah ee-lee een-teh-reh-see?*)

> **Idiomatic Expression:** "Свирка ми на ушите." -
> Meaning: "I don't care."
> (Literal translation: "It whistles in my ears.")

Making Plans

498.   Would you like to grab a coffee sometime?
Искаш ли някога да излезем за кафе?
(*Ees-kahsh lee nyah-koh-gah dah eez-leh-zehm zah kah-feh?*)

499. Let's plan a dinner outing this weekend.
Да планираме вечеря тази събота.
(*Dah plah-nee-rah-meh veh-cheh-ryah tah-zee suh-boh-tah.*)

500. How about going to a movie on Friday night?
Какво ще кажеш за филм в петък вечер?
(*Kahk-voh shteh kah-zhesh zah feelm v peh-tuhk veh-cher?*)

501. Do you want to join us for a hike next weekend?
Искаш ли да се присъединиш към нас за поход следващата събота?
(*Ees-kahsh lee dah seh prees-oo-eh-dee-neesh kuhm nahs zah poh-hod slehd-vah-shah-tah suh-boh-tah?*)

502. We should organize a game night soon.
Трябва да организираме игрална вечер скоро.
(*Tryahb-vah dah or-gah-nee-zee-rah-meh eeg-ral-nah veh-cher skoh-roh.*)

503. Let's catch up over lunch next week.
Да се срещнем на обяд следващата седмица.
(*Dah seh srehsh-nehm nah oh-byahd slehd-vah-shah-tah sehd-mee-tsah.*)

504. Would you be interested in a shopping trip?
Искаш ли да отидем на пазаруване?
(*Ees-kahsh lee dah oh-tee-dehm nah pah-zah-roo-vah-neh?*)

505. I'm thinking of visiting the museum; care to join?
Мисля да посетя музея; искаш ли да дойдеш?
(*Mees-lyah dah poh-seh-tyah moo-zey-ah; ees-kahsh lee dah doy-dehsh?*)

> **Idiomatic Expression:** "Не ми пука ни пет пари." -
> Meaning: "I don't care at all."
> (Literal translation: "I don't care even five cents.")

506. How about a picnic in the park?
Какво ще кажеш за пикник в парка?
(*Kahk-voh shteh kah-zhesh zah peek-neek v par-kah?*)

> **Fun Fact:** Bulgarian has a unique verb conjugation system, with various tenses, moods, and aspects.

507. Let's get together for a study session.
Нека се съберем за учебна сесия.
(*Neh-kah seh suh-beh-rem zah oo-cheb-nah seh-see-yah.*)

508. We should plan a beach day this summer.
Трябва да планираме плажен ден това лято.
(*Tryahb-vah dah plah-nee-rah-meh plah-zhen dehn toh-vah lyah-toh.*)

509. Want to come over for a barbecue at my place?
Искаш ли да дойдеш на барбекю при мен?
(*Ees-kahsh lee dah doy-dehsh nah bar-beh-kyoo pree men?*)

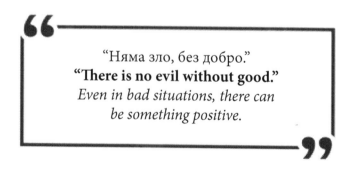

"Няма зло, без добро."
"There is no evil without good."
Even in bad situations, there can be something positive.

Interactive Challenge: Everyday Conversations
(Link each English word with their corresponding meaning in Bulgarian)

1) Conversation	Обмяна на мнения
2) Greeting	Обръщение
3) Question	Разговор
4) Answer	Реч
5) Salutation	Език
6) Communication	Дискусия
7) Dialogue	Диалог
8) Small Talk	Въпрос
9) Discussion	Комуникация
10) Speech	Поздрав
11) Language	Отговор
12) Exchange of Opinions	Неформален разговор
13) Expression	Малък разговор
14) Casual Conversation	Споделяне на идеи
15) Sharing Ideas	Изразяване

Correct Answers:

1. Conversation - Разговор
2. Greeting - Поздрав
3. Question - Въпрос
4. Answer - Отговор
5. Salutation - Обръщение
6. Communication - Комуникация
7. Dialogue - Диалог
8. Small Talk - Малък разговор
9. Discussion - Дискусия
10. Speech - Реч
11. Language - Език
12. Exchange of Opinions - Обмяна на мнения
13. Expression - Изразяване
14. Casual Conversation - Неформален разговор
15. Sharing Ideas - Споделяне на идеи

BUSINESS & WORK

- INTRODUCING YOURSELF IN A PROFESSIONAL SETTING -
- DISCUSSING WORK-RELATED TOPICS -
- NEGOTIATING BUSINESS DEALS OR CONTRACTS -

Professional Introductions

510. Hi, I'm [Your Name].
Здравей, аз съм [Твоето Име].
(*Zdrah-vey, az sum [Tvoh-eh-toh Ee-meh].*)

511. What do you do for a living?
Как си изкарваш прехраната?
(*Kahk see eez-kar-vash preh-hra-nah-tah?*)

512. What's your role in the company?
Каква е вашата роля в компанията?
(*Kahk-vah eh vah-shah-tah roh-lyah v kom-pah-nee-yah-tah?*)

513. Can you tell me about your background?
Можете ли да ми разкажете за вашето образование?
(*Mozh-eh-teh lee dah mee raz-kah-zheh-teh zah vah-sheh-toh oh-brah-zoh-vah-nee-eh?*)

514. This is my colleague, [Colleague's Name].
Това е моят колега, [Име на Колега].
(*Toh-vah eh moy-at ko-leh-gah, [Ee-meh nah Ko-leh-gah].*)

515. May I introduce myself?
Мога ли да се представя?
(*Moh-gah lee dah seh prehd-stah-vyah?*)

516. I work in [Your Department].
Работя в [Вашият Отдел].
(Rah-boh-tyah v [Vah-shee-yat Oht-del].)

517. How long have you been with the company?
От колко време сте в компанията?
(*Oht kol-koh vreh-meh steh v kom-pah-nee-yah-tah?*)

518. Are you familiar with our team?
Познавате ли нашия екип?
(*Pohz-nah-va-teh lee nah-shee-yah eh-keep?*)

519. Let me introduce you to our manager.
Нека ви запозная с нашия мениджър.
(*Neh-kah vee zah-poh-znah-yah s nah-shee-yah meh-nee-jur.*)

> **Travel Story:** At a traditional restaurant in Gabrovo, known for humor, a waiter joked, "Всеки смях носи щастие" (Every laugh brings happiness), illustrating the jovial spirit of the town.

Work Conversations

520. Can we discuss the project?
Можем ли да обсъдим проекта?
(*Mozh-em lee dah ob-suh-deem proh-ehk-tah?*)

521. Let's go over the details.
Да прегледаме детайлите.
(*Dah preh-gleh-dah-meh deh-tah-yee-teh.*)

522. What's the agenda for the meeting?
Каква е дневният ред за срещата?
(*Kahk-vah eh dnehv-nee-yaht red zah srehsh-tah-tah?*)

523. I'd like your input on this.
Искал бих да чуя вашето мнение по въпроса.
(*Ees-kahl bihkh dah choo-yah vah-sheh-toh mneh-nee-eh poh vuhp-roh-sah.*)

524. We need to address this issue.
Трябва да се занимаем с този проблем.
(*Tryab-va dah seh zah-nee-mah-em s toh-zee proh-blem.*)

525. How's the project progressing?
Как върви проектът?
(*Kahk vuhr-vi proh-ektuht?*)

526. Do you have any updates for me?
Имате ли някакви новини за мен?
(*Ee-mah-teh lee nyah-kah-kvee noh-vee-nee zah men?*)

527. Let's brainstorm some ideas.
Нека да съберем идеи.
(*Neh-kah dah suh-beh-rem ee-deh-ee.*)

528. Can we schedule a team meeting?
Можем ли да насрочим отборна среща?
(*Moh-zhem lee dah nah-sroh-cheem oht-bor-nah sreh-shtah?*)

529. I'm open to suggestions.
Отворен съм за предложения.
(*Oht-voh-ren suhm zah prehd-loh-zheh-nee-yah.*)

Business Negotiations

530. We need to negotiate the terms.
Трябва да преговорим условията.
(*Tryab-va dah preh-goh-voh-reem oos-loh-vee-yah-tah.*)

531. What's your offer?
Какво предлагате?
(*Kahk-voh prehd-lah-gah-teh?*)

532. Can we find a middle ground?
Можем ли да намерим компромис?
(*Moh-zhem lee dah nah-meh-reem kom-proh-meess?*)

> **Idiomatic Expression:** "Свалям шапка." -
> Meaning: "I am impressed or I respect that."
> (Literal translation: "I take off my hat.")

533. Let's discuss the contract.
Нека обсъдим договора.
(*Neh-kah ob-su-deem doh-goh-voh-rah.*)

534. Are you flexible on the price?
Гъвкави ли сте по отношение на цената?
(*Guhv-kah-vee lee steh poh oht-noh-sheh-nee-oh nah tseh-nah-tah?*)

535. I'd like to propose a deal.
Искам да предложа сделка.
(*Ee-skahm dah prehd-loh-zhah sdehl-kah.*)

536. We're interested in your terms.
Интересуват ни вашите условия.
(*Een-teh-reh-soo-vaht nee vah-shee-teh oos-loh-vee-yah.*)

537. Can we talk about the agreement?
Можем ли да говорим за споразумението?
(*Moh-zhem lee dah goh-voh-reem zah spoh-rah-zoo-meh-nee-eh-toh?*)

> **Fun Fact:** Bulgaria has a growing film industry with both historical and modern cinematic productions.

538.   Let's work out the details.
       Нека изясним детайлите.
       (*Neh-kah iz-yas-neem deh-tai-lee-teh.*)

539.   What are your conditions?
       Какви са вашите условия?
       (*Kahk-vee sah vah-shee-teh oo-sloh-vee-yah?*)

540.   We should reach a compromise.
       Трябва да постигнем компромис.
       (*Tryab-vah dah pohs-teeg-nem kom-proh-meess.*)

>   Fun Fact: Over the centuries, Bulgarian has evolved significantly, influenced by various historical events.

Workplace Etiquette

541.   Remember to be punctual.
       Не забравяйте да бъдете точни.
       (*Neh zah-brah-vai-teh dah buh-deh-teh tohch-nee.*)

542.   Always maintain a professional demeanor.
       Винаги поддържайте професионално поведение.
       (*Vee-nah-gee pohd-dur-zhai-teh proh-feh-see-oh-nahl-noh poh-veh-deh-nee-eh.*)

543.   Respect your colleagues' personal space.
       Уважавайте личното пространство на вашите колеги.
       (*Oo-vah-zhah-vai-teh leech-noh-toh prohs-trahn-stvoh nah vah-shee-teh koh-leh-gee.*)

>   Fun Fact: Traditional Bulgarian festivals often combine religious, seasonal, and historical themes.

544. Dress appropriately for the office.
Обличайте се подходящо за офиса.
(*Oh-blee-chai-teh seh pohd-hohd-yah-shoh zah oh-fees-ah.*)

545. Follow company policies and guidelines.
Спазвайте фирмените политики и насоки.
(*Spahz-vai-teh feer-meh-nee-teh poh-lee-tee-kee ee nah-soh-kee.*)

546. Use respectful language in conversations.
Използвайте уважителен език в разговорите.
(*Eez-pohlz-vai-teh oo-vah-zhee-teh-len eh-zihk v rahz-goh-voh-ree-teh.*)

547. Keep your workspace organized.
Поддържайте работното си място организирано.
(*Pohd-dur-zhai-teh rah-boht-noh-see miyah-stoh or-gah-nee-zee-rah-noh.*)

548. Be mindful of office noise levels.
Внимавайте на шумовете в офиса.
(*Vnee-mah-vai-teh nah shoo-moh-veh-teh v oh-fees-ah.*)

549. Offer assistance when needed.
Предлагайте помощ когато е необходимо.
(*Prehd-lah-gai-teh poh-mosht koh-gah-toh eh neh-ohb-hoh-dee-moh.*)

550. Practice good hygiene at work.
Спазвайте добра хигиена на работа.
(*Spahz-vai-teh doh-brah hi-gee-eh-nah nah rah-boh-tah.*)

551. Avoid office gossip and rumors.
Избягвайте клюкарството и слуховете в офиса.
(*Eez-biag-vai-teh klyoo-kar-stvoh-toh ee sloo-hoh-veh-teh v oh-fees-ah.*)

Job Interviews

552. Tell me about yourself.
      Разкажете ми за себе си.
      (Raz-kah-zheh-teh mee zah seh-beh see.)

553. What are your strengths and weaknesses?
      Какви са вашите силни и слаби страни?
      (Kahk-vee sah vah-shee-teh seel-nee ee slah-bee strah-nee?)

554. Describe your relevant experience.
      Опишете своя съответен опит.
      (Oh-pee-sheh-teh svoy-ah soo-ot-veh-ten oh-peet.)

555. Why do you want to work here?
      Защо искате да работите тук?
      (Zah-sh-toh ees-kah-teh dah rah-boh-tee-teh took?)

556. Where do you see yourself in five years?
      Къде се виждате след пет години?
      (Kuh-deh seh veezh-dah-teh sled peht goh-dee-nee?)

557. How do you handle challenges at work?
      Как се справяте с предизвикателствата на работа?
      (Kahk seh sprah-vyah-teh s preh-dee-zvee-kah-tehl-stvah-tah nah rah-boh-tah?)

558. What interests you about this position?
      Какво ви привлича в тази позиция?
      (Kahk-voh vee preev-leech-ah v tah-zee poh-zee-tsyah?)

559. Can you provide an example of your teamwork?
Можете ли да дадете пример за вашата екипна работа?
(*Moh-zheh-teh lee dah dah-deh-teh pree-mehr zah vah-shah-tah eh-keep-nah rah-boh-tah?*)

560. What motivates you in your career?
Какво ви мотивира в кариерата ви?
(*Kahk-voh vee moh-tee-vee-rah v kah-ree-eh-rah-tah vee?*)

561. Do you have any questions for us?
Имате ли въпроси за нас?
(*Ee-mah-teh lee vuh-proh-see zah nahs?*)

562. Thank you for considering me for the role.
Благодаря ви, че ме взехте предвид за тази роля.
(*Blah-go-dah-ryah vee, cheh meh vzeht-teh prehd-veed zah tah-zee roh-lyah.*)

Office Communication

563. Send me an email about it.
Изпратете ми имейл по въпроса.
(*Eez-prah-teh-teh mee ee-mayl poh vuh-proh-sah.*)

564. Let's schedule a conference call.
Да уговорим конферентен разговор.
(*Dah oo-goh-vo-reem kohn-feh-rehn-ten rahz-goh-vohr.*)

565. Could you clarify your message?
Можете ли да уточните съобщението си?
(*Moh-zheh-teh lee dah oo-toch-nee-teh soo-ob-sheh-nee-eh-toh see?*)

566. I'll forward the document to you.
Ще препратя документа до вас.
(*Shteh preh-prah-tyah doh-koo-men-tah doh vahs.*)

567. Please reply to this message.
Моля, отговорете на това съобщение.
(*Moh-lyah, ot-goh-voh-reh-teh nah toh-vah soo-ob-sheh-nee-eh.*)

568. We should have a team meeting.
Трябва да имаме отборна среща.
(*Tryahb-vah dah ee-mah-meh ot-bor-nah sreh-sh-tah.*)

> **Idiomatic Expression:** "Падам си по някого." -
> Meaning: "To have a crush on someone."
> (Literal translation: "I fall for someone.")

569. Check your inbox for updates.
Проверете входящата си поща за актуализации.
(*Proh-veh-reh-teh vhohd-yah-sh-tah see posh-tah zah
ak-too-ah-lee-zaht-see-ee.*)

570. I'll copy you on the correspondence.
Ще ви включа в кореспонденцията.
(*Shteh vee vkloo-chah v koh-rehs-pon-den-tsyah-tah.*)

571. I'll send you the meeting agenda.
Ще ви изпратя дневния ред на срещата.
(*Shteh vee eez-prah-tyah dnehv-nee-yah red nah sreh-sh-tah-tah.*)

572. Use the internal messaging system.
Използвайте вътрешната система за съобщения.
(*Eez-pohlz-vahy-teh vuh-trehsh-nah-tah sis-teh-mah zah
soo-ob-sheh-nee-yah.*)

573.   Keep everyone in the loop.
    Дръжте всички в течение.
    (*Druzh-teh vseech-kee v teh-cheh-nee-eh.*)

> "Няма дим без огън."
> **"There is no smoke without fire."**
> *If there are signs or rumors, there's likely some truth behind them.*

Cross Word Puzzle: Business & Work

(Provide the Bulgarian translation for the following English words)

Across

1. - CLIENT
4. - PROFESSIONAL
5. - INCOME
10. - MARKETING
11. - EMPLOYEE
12. - OFFICE
13. - SALARY

Down

2. - TEAM
3. - WORK
5. - CONTRACT
6. - SERVICE
7. - PROJECT
8. - BOSS
9. - BUSINESS
14. - PRODUCT

Correct Answers:

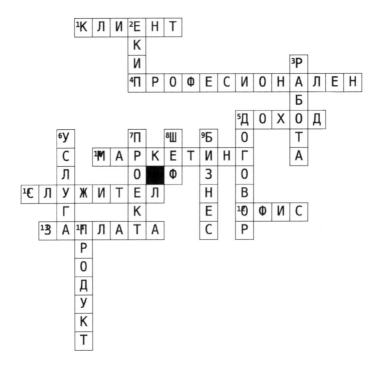

EVENTS & ENTERTAINMENT

- BUYING TICKETS FOR CONCERTS, MOVIES OR EVENTS -
- DISCUSSING ENTERTAINMENT & LEISURE ACTIVITIES -
- EXPRESSING JOY OR DISAPPOINTMENT WITH AN EVENT -

Ticket Purchases

574. I'd like to buy two tickets for the concert.
Искам да купя два билета за концерта.
(*Ees-kahm dah koop-yah dvah bee-leh-tah zah kon-tsehr-tah.*)

575. Can I get tickets for the movie tonight?
Мога ли да взема билети за филма тази вечер?
(*Moh-gah lee dah vze-mah bee-leh-tee zah feel-mah tah-zee veh-cher?*)

576. We need to book tickets for the upcoming event.
Трябва да резервираме билети за предстоящото събитие.
(*Tryab-vah dah reh-ze-rvee-rah-meh bee-leh-tee zah prehd-stoy-ahsh-toh soo-bee-tee-eh.*)

577. What's the price of admission?
Колко е входната такса?
(*Kohl-koh eh vhohd-nah-tah tahk-sah?*)

578. Do you offer any discounts for students?
Предлагате ли отстъпки за студенти?
(*Prehd-lah-gah-teh lee oht-stuhp-kee zah stoo-den-tee?*)

579. Are there any available seats for the matinee?
Има ли свободни места за матинето?
(*Ee-mah lee svoh-bohd-nee mehs-tah zah mah-tee-neh-toh?*)

580. How can I purchase tickets online?
Как мога да закупя билети онлайн?
(*Kahk moh-gah dah zah-koop-yah bee-leh-tee on-line?*)

581. Is there a box office nearby?
Има ли близка каса?
(*Ee-mah lee blees-kah kah-sah?*)

582. Are tickets refundable if I can't attend?
Възстановими ли са билетите, ако не мога да присъствам?
(*Vuhz-stoh-nah-vee-mee lee sah bee-leh-tee-teh, ah-koh neh moh-gah dah pree-suh-stvahm?*)

583. Can I choose my seats for the show?
Мога ли да избера местата си за представлението?
(*Moh-gah lee dah eez-beh-rah mehs-tah-tah see zah prehd-stah-vleh-nee-eh-toh?*)

584. Can I reserve tickets for the theater?
Мога ли да резервирам билети за театъра?
(*Moh-gah lee dah reh-ze-rvee-rahm bee-leh-tee zah teh-ah-too-rah?*)

585. How early should I buy event tickets?
Колко рано трябва да купя билети за събитието?
(*Kohl-koh rah-noh tryab-vah dah koop-yah bee-leh-tee zah soo-bee-tee-eh-toh?*)

586. Are there any VIP packages available?
Има ли налични VIP пакети?
(*Ee-mah lee nah-leech-nee Vee-ee-peh pah-keh-tee?*)

587. What's the seating arrangement like?
Каква е подредбата на седалките?
(*Kah-kvah eh poh-dreh-dbah-tah nah sehd-ahl-kee-teh?*)

> **Idiomatic Expression:** "Да си обереш кашата." -
> Meaning: "To face the consequences."
> (Literal translation: "To pick up your mess.")

588. Is there a family discount for the movie?
Има ли семейна отстъпка за филма?
(*Ee-mah lee seh-mey-na oht-stuhp-kah zah feel-mah?*)

589. I'd like to purchase tickets for my friends.
Искам да купя билети за моите приятели.
(*Ees-kahm dah koop-yah bee-leh-tee zah moy-teh pree-ya-te-lee.*)

> **Fun Fact:** Bulgaria's diverse ecosystems are home to a variety of wildlife, including wolves and bears.

590. Do they accept credit cards for tickets?
Приемат ли кредитни карти за билети?
(*Pree-eh-maht lee kreh-deet-nee kar-tee zah bee-leh-tee?*)

591. Are there any age restrictions for entry?
Има ли възрастови ограничения за входа?
(*Ee-mah lee vuhz-rah-sto-vi oh-grah-nee-cheh-nee-ya zah vho-dah?*)

592. Can I exchange my ticket for a different date?
Мога ли да сменим билета си за друга дата?
(*Moh-gah lee dah smeh-neem bee-leh-tah see zah droo-gah dah-tah?*)

Leisure Activities

593. What do you feel like doing this weekend?
Какво искаш да правим този уикенд?
(*Kahk-voh ees-kahsh dah prah-veem toh-zee oo-ee-kehnd?*)

594. Let's discuss our entertainment options.
Нека обсъдим нашите възможности за забавление.
(*Neh-kah ob-suh-deem nah-shee-teh vuhz-mohzh-nos-tee zah zah-bav-leh-nee-eh.*)

> **Fun Fact:** The National Revival period was a significant era of cultural and national awakening in Bulgaria.

595. I'm planning a leisurely hike on Saturday.
Планирам спокойно изкачване в събота.
(*Plah-nee-rahm spoh-koy-noh ees-kahch-vah-neh v suh-boh-tah.*)

596. Do you enjoy outdoor activities like hiking?
Харесвате ли активности на открито като планинарство?
(*Hah-rehs-va-teh lee ak-tee-vnos-tee nah oht-kree-toh kah-toh plah-nee-nahr-stvoh?*)

597. Have you ever tried indoor rock climbing?
Опитвал ли си някога скално катерене на закрито?
(*Oh-pee-tvahl lee see nyah-koh-gah skahl-noh kah-teh-reh-neh nah zah-kree-toh?*)

598. I'd like to explore some new hobbies.
Искам да опитам някои нови хобита.
(*Ees-kahm dah oh-pee-tahm nyah-koy noh-vee hoh-bee-tah.*)

599. What are your favorite pastimes?
Какви са любимите ти занимания?
(*Kahk-vee sah lyoo-bee-mee-teh tee zah-nee-mah-nee-ya?*)

> **Cultural Insight:** Plovdiv, one of the oldest cities in Europe, boasts a rich history with Thracian, Greek, Roman, and Ottoman influences.

600. Are there any interesting events in town?
Има ли интересни събития в града?
(*Ee-mah lee een-teh-res-nee suh-bee-tee-ya v grah-dah?*)

601. Let's check out the local art exhibition.
Нека разгледаме местната художествена изложба.
(*Neh-kah rahz-gleh-dah-meh mehs-tnah-tah hoo-doh-zhes-tveh-nah eez-lozh-bah.*)

602. How about attending a cooking class?
Какво ще кажете за кулинарен курс?
(*Kahk-voh shteh kah-zheh-teh zah koo-lee-nah-ren koors?*)

603. Let's explore some new recreational activities.
Нека проучим нови развлекателни дейности.
(*Neh-kah proh-oo-cheem noh-vee raz-vleh-kah-tel-nee dey-nos-tee.*)

604. What's your go-to leisure pursuit?
Какво е твоето любимо свободно време занимание?
(*Kahk-voh eh tvoh-eh-toh lyoo-bee-moh svoh-bod-noh vreh-meh zah-nee-mah-nee-eh?*)

605. I'm considering trying a new hobby.
Обмислям да опитам ново хоби.
(*Ob-meese-lyahm dah oh-pee-tahm noh-voh hoh-bee.*)

606. Have you ever attended a painting workshop?
Ходил/а ли си някога на живописен семинар?
(*Hoh-deel/ah lee see nyah-koh-gah nah zhih-vo-pee-sen seh-mee-nahr?*)

> **Fun Fact:** Bulgarian names typically consist of a first name, a paternal name, and a family name.

607. What's your favorite way to unwind?
Какъв е твоят любим начин за отдих?
(*Kah-kuv eh tvoh-yaht lyoo-beem nah-cheen zah oht-deeh?*)

608. I'm interested in joining a local club.
Интересувам се да се присъединя към местен клуб.
(*Een-teh-reh-soo-vahm seh dah seh prees-uh-eh-dee-nyah kuhm mehs-ten kloob.*)

609. Let's plan a day filled with leisure.
Нека планираме ден, изпълнен с отдих.
(*Neh-kah plah-nee-rah-meh dehn, ees-puhl-nen s oht-deeh.*)

610. Have you ever been to a live comedy show?
Ходил/а ли си някога на живо комедийно шоу?
(*Hoh-deel/ah lee see nyah-koh-gah nah zhih-voh koh-meh-dee-y-noh show?*)

611. I'd like to attend a cooking demonstration.
Искам да посетя кулинарна демонстрация.
(*Ees-kahm dah poh-seh-tyah koo-lee-nahr-nah deh-mohn-strah-tsee-ya.*)

> **Fun Fact:** There are several distinct dialects in Bulgarian, each with its own peculiarities in pronunciation and vocabulary.

Event Reactions

612. That concert was amazing! I loved it!
Този концерт беше страхотен! Много ми хареса!
(*Toh-zee kon-tzehrt beh-sheh strah-ho-ten! Mnoh-goh mee hah-reh-sah!*)

139

613. I had such a great time at the movie.
Имах страхотно време на филма.
(*Ee-mahkh strah-hot-noh vreh-meh nah feel-mah.*)

614. The event exceeded my expectations.
Събитието надмина очакванията ми.
(*Suh-bee-tee-e-toh nahd-mee-nah oh-chak-vah-nee-ah-tah mee.*)

615. I was thrilled by the performance.
Представлението ме възхити.
(*Prehd-stahv-leh-nee-e-toh meh vuhz-khee-tee.*)

616. It was an unforgettable experience.
Това беше незабравимо преживяване.
(*Toh-vah beh-sheh neh-zah-brah-vee-moh preh-zhih-vyah-vah-neh.*)

617. I can't stop thinking about that show.
Не мога да спра да мисля за това предаване.
(*Neh moh-gah dah sprah dah mees-lyah zah toh-vah preh-dah-vah-neh.*)

618. Unfortunately, the event was a letdown.
За съжаление, събитието беше разочароващо.
(*Zah suh-zhah-leh-nee-eh, suh-bee-tee-e-toh beh-sheh rah-zoh-chah-roh-vahsh-toh.*)

619. I was disappointed with the movie.
Разочарован съм от филма.
(*Rah-zoh-chah-roh-vahn suhm oht feel-mah.*)

620. The concert didn't meet my expectations.
Концертът не отговори на очакванията ми.
(*Kon-tzehrt-uht neh oht-goh-vo-ree nah oh-chak-vah-nee-ah-tah mee.*)

621.   I expected more from the exhibition.
Очаквах повече от изложбата.
(*Oh-chak-vahkh poh-veh-cheh oht eez-lozh-bah-tah.*)

622.   The event left me speechless; it was superb!
Събитието ме остави без думи; беше превъзходно!
(*Suh-bee-tee-e-toh meh oh-stah-vee behz doo-mee; beh-sheh preh-vuhz-hod-noh!*)

623.   I was absolutely thrilled with the performance.
Изключително бях впечатлен/а от представлението.
(*Eez-klyoo-chee-tehl-noh byah vpeh-chat-lehn/ah oht prehd-stahv-leh-nee-e-toh.*)

624.   The movie was a pleasant surprise.
Филмът беше приятна изненада.
(*Feel-muht beh-sheh pree-yat-nah eez-neh-nah-dah.*)

625.   I had such a blast at the exhibition.
Изкарах страхотно на изложбата.
(*Eez-kah-rahkh strah-hot-noh nah eez-lozh-bah-tah.*)

626.   The concert was nothing short of fantastic.
Концертът беше нищо по-малко от фантастичен.
(*Kon-tzehrt-uht beh-sheh neesh-toh poh-mahl-koh oht fahn-tahs-tee-chehn.*)

627.   I'm still on cloud nine after the event.
Още съм на седмото небе след събитието.
(*Oh-shteh suhm nah sehd-moh-toh neh-beh slehd suh-bee-tee-e-toh.*)

> **Travel Story:** In the Belogradchik Rocks, a guide remarked, "Природата е най-добрият художник" (Nature is the best artist), admiring the natural rock formations.

628. I was quite underwhelmed by the show.
Шоуто ме разочарова доста.
(*Show-to me razo-cha-ro-va dos-ta.*)

629. I expected more from the movie.
Очаквах повече от филма.
(*O-chak-vah po-ve-che ot fil-ma.*)

630. Unfortunately, the exhibition didn't impress me.
За съжаление, изложбата не ме впечатли.
(*Za sa-zha-le-nie, iz-lozh-ba-ta ne me vpe-cha-tli.*)

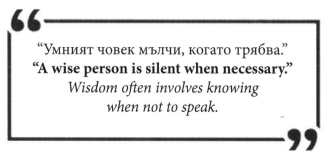

"Умният човек мълчи, когато трябва."
"A wise person is silent when necessary."
*Wisdom often involves knowing
when not to speak.*

Mini Lesson:
Basic Grammar Principles in Bulgarian #2

Introduction:

In this second installment of our Bulgarian grammar series, we delve deeper into the linguistic intricacies of this South Slavic language. Building on our previous lesson, we'll explore more elements that are crucial for both spoken and written Bulgarian.

1. Verb Tenses:

Bulgarian verbs express various tenses, including present, past (aorist and imperfect), and future. The formation of these tenses is essential for effective communication.

- *Present: Чета книга. (I read a book.)*
- *Aorist (simple past): Прочетох книга. (I read a book.)*
- *Imperfect (past continuous): Четях книга. (I was reading a book.)*
- *Future: Ще прочета книга. (I will read a book.)*

2. Aspect:

In Bulgarian, verbs can be imperfective (actions that are ongoing or repeated) or perfective (completed actions).

- *Imperfective: Пиша писмо. (I am writing a letter/I write letters.)*
- *Perfective: Напиша писмо. (I wrote a letter.)*

3. Mood:

Bulgarian verbs express different moods, including indicative, imperative, and conditional.

- *Indicative: Той отива на работа. (He goes to work.)*
- *Imperative: Иди на работа! (Go to work!)*
- *Conditional: Бих отишъл на работа. (I would go to work.)*

4. Reflexive Verbs:

Some Bulgarian verbs are reflexive, indicating that the action reflects back on the subject.

- *Обличам се. (I dress myself.)*

5. Passive Voice:

Passive voice in Bulgarian is formed with a specific set of verb forms or by using the verb "бъда" (to be) with a past participle.

- *Книгата е написана. (The book is written.)*

6. Adverbs:

Adverbs modify verbs, adjectives, or other adverbs and are essential for describing how, where, or when something happens.

- *Бързо бяга. (He runs quickly.)*

7. Prepositions and Postpositions:

Bulgarian uses prepositions and postpositions to show the relationship between words.

- *Преди обяд. (Before noon.)*
- *След училище. (After school.)*

Conclusion:

Understanding these grammatical aspects enhances your ability to construct meaningful and nuanced sentences in Bulgarian. Practice regularly by engaging with native speakers and consuming Bulgarian media to achieve proficiency. Успех! (Good luck!)

HEALTHCARE & MEDICAL NEEDS

- EXPLAINING SYMPTOMS TO A DOCTOR -
- REQUESTING MEDICAL ASSISTANCE -
- DISCUSSING MEDICATIONS AND TREATMENT -

Explaining Symptoms

631. I have a persistent headache.
Имам постоянна главоболие.
(Ee-mam pos-to-yahn-na gla-vo-bo-li-e.)

632. My throat has been sore for a week.
От седмица имам болки в гърлото.
(Ot sed-mee-tsa ee-mam bol-ki v gur-lo-to.)

633. I've been experiencing stomach pain and nausea.
Имам болки в стомаха и гадене.
(Ee-mam bol-ki v sto-ma-ha i ga-de-ne.)

634. I have a high fever and chills.
Имам висока треска и озноб.
(Ee-mam vi-so-ka tres-ka i oz-nob.)

635. My back has been hurting for a few days.
От няколко дни ме боли гърбът.
(Ot nya-kol-ko dni me bo-li gurbut.)

636. I'm coughing up yellow mucus.
Кашлям жълт храчки.
(Kash-lyam zhalt hrahch-ki.)

637. I have a rash on my arm.
Имам обрив по ръката.
(Ee-mam o-breev po ruk-a-ta.)

Fun Fact: Saints Cyril and Methodius, the creators of the Cyrillic alphabet, are celebrated in Bulgaria.

638. I've been having trouble breathing.
Имам затруднения с дишането.
(*Ee-mam za-trud-ne-ni-ya s dish-a-ne-to.*)

639. I feel dizzy and lightheaded.
Чувствам замаяност и лекота.
(*Choov-stvam za-ma-ya-nost i le-kota.*)

640. My joints are swollen and painful.
Ставите ми са подути и болезнени.
(*Sta-vi-te mi sa po-du-ti i bo-lez-ne-ni.*)

641. I've had diarrhea for two days.
От два дни имам диария.
(*Ot dva dni ee-mam di-a-ri-ya.*)

642. My eyes are red and itchy.
Очите ми са червени и сърбят.
(*O-chi-te mi sa cher-ve-ni i sur-byat.*)

643. I've been vomiting since last night.
Повръщам от снощи.
(*Po-vrash-tam ot sno-shti.*)

644. I have a painful, persistent toothache.
Имам болезнена и постоянна зъбобол.
(*Ee-mam bo-lez-ne-na i pos-to-yahn-na zab-o-bol.*)

645. I'm experiencing fatigue and weakness.
Чувствам умора и слабост.
(*Choov-stvam oo-mo-ra i sla-bost.*)

646. I've noticed blood in my urine.
Има кръв в урината ми.
(*Ee-mah kruv v oo-ree-nah-tah mee.*)

647. My nose is congested, and I can't smell anything.
Носът ми е запушен и не усещам миризми.
(*No-suh-t mee eh zah-poosh-en ee neh oo-seh-sham mee-reez-mee.*)

648. I have a cut that's not healing properly.
Имам рана, която не зараства правилно.
(*Ee-mah rah-nah, koy-ah-toh neh zah-rah-stah-vah prah-veel-no.*)

649. My ears have been hurting, and I can't hear well.
Ушите ми болят и не чувам добре.
(*Oo-shee-teh mee boh-lyat ee neh choo-vam doh-breh.*)

650. I think I might have a urinary tract infection.
Мисля, че имам инфекция на пикочните пътища.
(*Mees-lya, cheh ee-mam een-fek-tsi-ya nah pee-koch-nee-te poo-teeshta.*)

651. I've had trouble sleeping due to anxiety.
Имам проблеми със съня заради тревожност.
(*Ee-mam proh-blem-ee sus sun-ya zah-rah-dee treh-vohzh-nost.*)

Requesting Medical Assistance

652. I need to see a doctor urgently.
Спешно ми трябва да видя лекар.
(*Spehsh-noh mee tryab-vah dah vee-dyah leh-kar.*)

653. Can you call an ambulance, please?
Можете ли да повикате линейка, моля?
(*Moh-zheh-teh lee dah poh-vee-kah-teh lee-ney-kah, moh-lya?*)

> **Travel Story:** At a historical reenactment in Shumen, an
> actor said, "Историята оживява тук" (History comes
> alive here), bringing the past into the present.

654. I require immediate medical attention.
Нуждая се от незабавна медицинска помощ.
(*Noozh-dah-ya seh ot neh-zah-bav-nah meh-dee-tsin-skah
poh-mosht.*)

655. Is there an available appointment today?
Има ли свободен час за днес?
(*Ee-mah lee svoh-boh-den chahs zah dnes?*)

656. Please help me find a nearby clinic.
Моля, помогнете ми да намеря близка клиника.
(*Moh-lya, poh-mohg-neh-teh mee dah nah-meh-ryah blees-kah
klee-nee-kah.*)

657. I think I'm having a medical emergency.
Мисля, че имам медицинска спешност.
(*Mees-lya, cheh ee-mam meh-dee-tsin-skah spehsh-nost.*)

658. Can you recommend a specialist?
Можете ли да препоръчате специалист?
(*Moh-zheh-teh lee dah preh-poh-ruh-cha-teh speh-tsee-ah-leest?*)

659. I'm in severe pain; can I see a doctor now?
Имам силни болки; мога ли да видя лекар сега?
(*Ee-mam seel-nee bohl-kee; moh-gah lee dah vee-dyah leh-kar
seh-gah?*)

660. Is there a 24-hour pharmacy in the area?
Има ли 24-часова аптека в района?
(Ee-ma lee dvah-deset ee chetiri chah-soh-vah ap-teh-kah v rai-yo-nah?)

661. I need a prescription refill.
Трябва ми попълнение на рецепта.
(Tryab-va mee po-puhl-ne-nee-eh na re-tsep-tah.)

662. Can you guide me to the nearest hospital?
Можете ли да ме насочите към най-близката болница?
(Moh-zheh-teh lee dah meh nah-soh-chee-teh kuhm nai-blee-zkah-tah bol-nee-tsah?)

663. I've cut myself and need medical assistance.
Порязах се и имам нужда от медицинска помощ.
(Poh-riah-zahh seh ee ee-mam noozh-dah ot meh-dee-tseen-skah poh-mosht.)

664. My child has a high fever; what should I do?
Детето ми има висока температура; какво трябва да направя?
(Deh-teh-toh mee ee-mah vee-soh-kah tehm-peh-rah-too-rah; kahk-voh tryab-vah dah nah-prah-vyah?)

665. Is there a walk-in clinic nearby?
Има ли клиника без предварително записване в района?
(Ee-mah lee klee-nee-kah behz prehd-vah-ree-tehl-noh zah-pee-svah-neh v rai-yo-nah?)

666. I need medical advice about my condition.
Трябва ми медицински съвет за състоянието ми.
(Tryab-vah mee meh-dee-tseen-skee suh-vet zah suh-stoy-ah-nee-eh-toh mee.)

667. My medication has run out; I need a refill.
Лекарствата ми свършиха; трябва ми попълнение.
(*Leh-kahr-stvah-tah mee svuhr-shee-hah; tryab-vah mee po-puhl-ne-nee-eh.*)

668. Can you direct me to an eye doctor?
Можете ли да ме насочите към очен лекар?
(*Moh-zheh-teh lee dah meh nah-soh-chee-teh kuhm oh-chen leh-kahr?*)

669. I've been bitten by a dog; I'm concerned.
Куче ме ухапа; притеснявам се.
(*Koo-cheh meh oo-hah-pah; pree-tehs-nyah-vam seh.*)

670. Is there a dentist available for an emergency?
Има ли достъпен зъболекар за спешни случаи?
(*Ee-mah lee doh-stuh-pen zuh-boh-leh-kahr zah spehsh-nee sloo-chai?*)

671. I think I might have food poisoning.
Мисля, че имам хранително отравяне.
(*Mees-lya, cheh ee-mah hrah-nee-tel-noh o-trah-vyah-neh.*)

672. Can you help me find a pediatrician for my child?
Можете ли да ми помогнете да намеря педиатър за детето ми?
(*Moh-zheh-teh lee dah mee poh-mohg-neh-teh dah nah-meh-ryah peh-dee-a-tuhr zah deh-teh-toh mee?*)

> **Idiomatic Expression:** "Оставам с клюн." -
> Meaning: "To be surprised or speechless."
> (Literal translation: "I'm left with a beak.")

Discussing Medications and Treatments

673. What is this medication for?
За какво е това лекарство?
(Zah kah-kvoh eh toh-vah leh-kar-stvoh?)

674. How often should I take this pill?
Колко често трябва да приемам тази хапче?
(Kohl-koh cheh-stoh tryab-vah dah pree-eh-mahm tah-zee hahp-cheh?)

675. Are there any potential side effects?
Има ли потенциални странични ефекти?
(Ee-mah lee poh-ten-tsi-ahl-nee strah-neech-nee eh-fek-tee?)

676. Can I take this medicine with food?
Мога ли да приемам това лекарство с храна?
(Moh-gah lee dah pree-eh-mahm toh-vah leh-kar-stvoh s hrah-nah?)

677. Should I avoid alcohol while on this medication?
Трябва ли да избягвам алкохола при прием на това лекарство?
(Tryab-vah lee dah eez-byahg-vahm al-koh-hoh-lah pree pree-ehm nah toh-vah leh-kar-stvoh?)

678. Is it safe to drive while taking this?
Безопасно ли е да шофирам, докато приемам това лекарство?
(Beh-zoh-pahs-noh lee eh dah shoh-fee-rahm, doh-kah-toh pree-eh-mahm toh-vah leh-kar-stvoh?)

679. Are there any dietary restrictions?
Има ли диетични ограничения?
(Ee-mah lee dee-eh-teech-nee oh-grah-neech-ehn-ee-yah?)

680. Can you explain the dosage instructions?
Можете ли да обясните инструкциите за дозиране?
(Moh-zheh-teh lee dah ob-yahs-nee-teh een-struhk-tsee-ee-teh zah doh-zee-rah-neh?)

681. What should I do if I miss a dose?
Какво трябва да направя, ако пропусна доза?
(Kahk-voh tryab-vah dah nah-prah-vyah ah-koh proh-poos-nah doh-zah?)

682. How long do I need to continue this treatment?
Колко време трябва да продължа това лечение?
(Kohl-koh vreh-meh tryab-vah dah proh-dool-zhah toh-vah leh-cheh-nee-eh?)

683. Can I get a generic version of this medication?
Мога ли да получа генерична версия на това лекарство?
(Moh-gah lee dah poh-loo-chah geh-neh-reesh-nah vehr-see-yah nah toh-vah leh-kar-stvoh?)

684. Is there a non-prescription alternative?
Има ли алтернатива без рецепта?
(Ee-mah lee ahl-tehr-nah-tee-vah behz reh-tsep-tah?)

685. How should I store this medication?
Как трябва да съхранявам това лекарство?
(Kahk tryab-vah dah suh-hrahn-yah-vahm toh-vah leh-kar-stvoh?)

686. Can you show me how to use this inhaler?
Можете ли да ми покажете как се използва този инхалатор?
(Moh-zheh-teh lee dah mee poh-kah-zheh-teh kahk seh eez-pohlz-vah toh-zee een-hah-lah-tor?)

687. What's the expiry date of this medicine?
Каква е срокът на годност на това лекарство?
(*Kah-kvah eh sroh-kut nah gohd-nost nah toh-vah leh-kar-stvoh?*)

> **Fun Fact:** Traditional Bulgarian folk music is recognized for its unique, complex rhythms.

688. Do I need to finish the entire course of antibiotics?
Трябва ли да завърша целия курс на антибиотици?
(*Tryab-vah lee dah zah-vur-shah tseh-lee-yah koors nah ahn-tee-bee-oh-tee-tsee?*)

689. Can I cut these pills in half?
Мога ли да разделя тези таблетки на половина?
(*Moh-gah lee dah rahz-deh-lyah teh-zee tah-bleht-kee nah poh-loh-vee-nah?*)

690. Is there an over-the-counter pain reliever you recommend?
Препоръчвате ли някой безрецептен обезболяващ?
(*Preh-poh-ruhch-vah-teh lee nyah-koy behz-reh-tsep-ten oh-behz-boh-lyah-vahsht?*)

691. Can I take this medication while pregnant?
Мога ли да приемам това лекарство по време на бременност?
(*Moh-gah lee dah pree-eh-mahm toh-vah leh-kar-stvoh poh vreh-meh nah breh-mehn-nost?*)

692. What should I do if I experience an allergic reaction?
Какво трябва да направя, ако имам алергична реакция?
(*Kahk-voh tryab-vah dah nah-prah-vyah ah-koh ee-mahm ah-ler-geechnah reh-ahk-tsee-yah?*)

> **Fun Fact:** The ancient city of Nesebar, a UNESCO World Heritage site, is known for its rich history and architecture.

693. Can you provide more information about this treatment plan?
Можете ли да предоставите повече информация за този лечебен план?

(Moh-zheh-teh lee dah preh-doh-stah-vee-teh poh-veh-cheh een-for-mah-tsee-yah zah toh-zee leh-cheh-ben plan?)

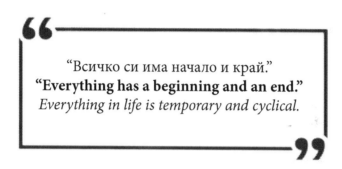

"Всичко си има начало и край."
"Everything has a beginning and an end."
Everything in life is temporary and cyclical.

Word Search Puzzle: Healthcare

HOSPITAL
БОЛНИЦА
DOCTOR
ЛЕКАР
MEDICINE
ЛЕКАРСТВО
PRESCRIPTION
РЕЦЕПТА
APPOINTMENT
ЧАС
SURGERY
ХИРУРГИЯ
VACCINE
ВАКСИНА
PHARMACY
АПТЕКА
ILLNESS
БОЛЕСТ
TREATMENT
ЛЕЧЕНИЕ
DIAGNOSIS
ДИАГНОЗА
RECOVERY
ВЪЗСТАНОВЯВАНЕ
SYMPTOM
СИМПТОМ
IMMUNIZATION
ИМУНИЗАЦИЯ

```
P Z K F R P H A R M A C Y E Q
R A X Z S H Ч G A E T X Y N B
E Z K Z Z A D Z J N K I H I U
T X J E C F Q I O I V A I C I
V T N H Л N N Y G C N K J C L
P R E S C R I P T I O N A A L
C И T E M T H G S E I I P B E
T H H F Z И Y Y K M R S O Ъ S
T Я D E C Y M F V E Б O I З S
O C И K Ч P P K J O U N N C Q
I P A Г T E Б U Л U O G T T J
A B Y O P O Л H D I C A M A Y
T П M L Л У И M T K O I E H W
G A T E P Ц P A L B S D N O G
O D C E A E Z И T S Z R T B A
W T C T K I Ц C X F K P D Я H
V C Q C N A P E B L Q Z C B O
L S G U A A F X П J F Q C A S
U V M Q K E R C K T N S З H P
F M M E Q T D C P Y A O K E I
I T Л У R E G R U S H T I M T
T N E M T A E R T Г E C P I A
R E C O V E R Y A N U E G F L
E P V B I I U И R O T C O D M
N E N E A E Д M O T П M И C X
И M У H И З A Ц И Я V P W N Q
H D I B Z S I K Z S V S T M W
D S U B U D E C D H I Q T N N
W P V U R B J W K R N O X C M
```

158

Correct Answers:

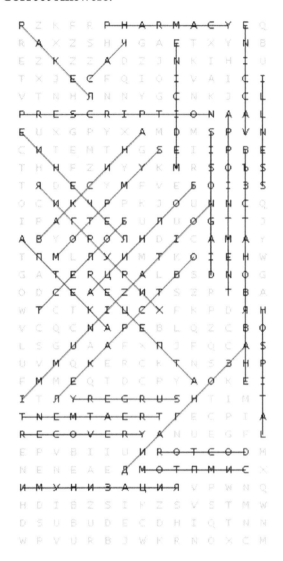

FAMILY & RELATIONSHIPS

- TALKING ABOUT FAMILY MEMBERS & RELATIONSHIPS -
- DISCUSSING PERSONAL LIFE & EXPERIENCES -
- EXPRESSING EMOTIONS & SENTIMENTS -

Family Members and Relationships

694. He's my younger brother.
Той е моят по-малък брат.
(Toy eh moyat po-ma-luhk brat.)

695. She's my cousin from my mother's side.
Тя е моята братовчедка от майчина страна.
(Tyah eh moyata bra-toh-vched-kah ot may-chee-na stra-na.)

696. My grandparents have been married for 50 years.
Моите баба и дядо са женени от 50 години.
(Moy-teh bah-bah ee dyah-doh sa zheh-ne-nee ot peh-tdeh-seht goh-dee-nee.)

697. We're like sisters from another mister.
Ние сме като сестри, но от различен баща.
(Nee-eh sme kah-toh ses-tri, noh ot raz-lee-chen bah-sh-tah.)

698. He's my husband's best friend.
Той е най-добрият приятел на моя съпруг.
(Toy eh nay-doh-bree-yat pree-ya-tel na moy-ya suh-proog.)

699. She's my niece on my father's side.
Тя е моята племенница от бащина страна.
(Tyah eh moyata pleh-men-nee-tsah ot bahsh-tee-na stra-na.)

700. They are my in-laws.
Те са моите свекърви и свекър.
(Teh sa moy-teh sve-kur-vi ee sve-kur.)

701. Our family is quite close-knit.
Нашето семейство е много сплотено.
(Nah-she-toh seh-my-yes-tvoh eh mnogo sploh-teh-noh.)

702. He's my adopted son.
Той е моят осиновен син.
(Toy eh moyat o-see-no-vehn seen.)

703. She's my half-sister.
Тя е моята полусестра.
(Tyah eh moyata po-lu-ses-trah.)

> **Travel Story:** In a traditional house in Melnik, a hostess declared, "Нашият дом е нашата крепост" (Our home is our fortress), showcasing Bulgarian hospitality.

704. My parents are divorced.
Моите родители са разведени.
(Moy-teh roh-dee-teh-lee sa raz-veh-deh-nee.)

705. He's my fiancé.
Той е моят годеник.
(Toy eh moyat goh-deh-neek.)

706. She's my daughter-in-law.
Тя е моята снаха.
(Tyah eh moyata sna-ha.)

> **Idiomatic Expression:** "Хапва ми се нещо." - Meaning: "I feel like eating something."
> (Literal translation: "Something bites me.")

707. We're childhood friends.
Ние сме детски приятели.
(*Nee-eh sme deht-ski pree-ya-teh-lee.*)

708. My twin brother and I are very close.
Аз и моят близнак сме много близки.
(*Az ee moyat bleez-nak sme mnogo bleez-kee.*)

709. He's my godfather.
Той е моят кръстник.
(*Toy eh moyat krus-tnik.*)

710. She's my stepsister.
Тя е моята доведена сестра.
(*Tyah eh moyata doh-veh-deh-nah ses-trah.*)

711. My aunt is a world traveler.
Моята леля е световен пътешественик.
(*Moyata leh-lya eh sve-toh-ven poo-teh-shest-veh-neek.*)

712. We're distant relatives.
Ние сме далечни роднини.
(*Nee-eh sme da-lech-nee rohd-nee-nee.*)

713. He's my brother-in-law.
Той е моят зет.
(*Toy eh moyat zet.*)

714. She's my ex-girlfriend.
Тя е моята бивша приятелка.
(*Tyah eh moyata beev-shah pree-ya-tel-kah.*)

Personal Life and Experiences

715. I've traveled to over 20 countries.
Посетил съм над 20 държави.
(Poh-seh-teel sum nad dvah-dyeset dur-zha-vee.)

716. She's an avid hiker and backpacker.
Тя е страстна туристка и бекпекърка.
(Tyah eh strahst-nah too-reest-kah ee bek-pek-ur-kah.)

717. I enjoy cooking and trying new recipes.
Обичам да готвя и да пробвам нови рецепти.
(Oh-bee-cham dah goht-vya ee dah proh-bvam noh-vee reh-tsep-tee.)

718. He's a professional photographer.
Той е професионален фотограф.
(Toy eh proh-feh-see-oh-nah-len foh-toh-grahf.)

719. I'm passionate about environmental conservation.
Аз съм страстен защитник на околната среда.
(Az sum strahs-ten zah-shtiht-neek nah oh-kohl-nah-tah sreh-dah.)

720. She's a proud dog owner.
Тя е горда собственичка на куче.
(Tyah eh gorr-dah sob-stveh-neech-kah nah koo-cheh.)

721. I love attending live music concerts.
Обожавам да посещавам концерти на жива музика.
(Oh-boh-zha-vam dah poh-seh-shtah-vam kohn-tser-tee nah zhee-vah moo-zee-kah.)

722. He's an entrepreneur running his own business.
Той е предприемач, който управлява собствения си бизнес.
(*Toy eh prehd-pree-eh-mach, koy-toh oo-prav-lyah-va sohb-stveh-nee-ya see beez-nes.*)

723. I've completed a marathon.
Завърших маратон.
(*Zah-vur-sheeh mah-rah-ton.*)

724. She's a dedicated volunteer at a local shelter.
Тя е отдаден доброволец в местно убежище.
(*Tyah eh oht-dah-den doh-broh-voh-lets v mehs-t-noh oo-beh-zheesh-teh.*)

725. I'm a history buff.
Аз съм ентусиаст по история.
(*Az sum en-too-see-ahst poh is-toh-ree-ya.*)

726. I'm a proud parent of three children.
Аз съм горд родител на трима деца.
(*Az sum gohrd roh-dee-tel nah tree-mah deh-tsa.*)

727. I've recently taken up painting.
Наскоро започнах да рисувам.
(*Nah-sko-roh zah-pohch-nah dah ree-soo-vahm.*)

728. She's a film enthusiast.
Тя е филмов ентусиаст.
(*Tyah eh feel-mohv en-too-see-ahst.*)

729. I enjoy gardening in my free time.
Обичам да се занимавам с градинарство в свободното си време.
(*Oh-bee-cham dah seh zah-nee-mah-vahm s grah-dee-nar-stvoh v svoh-bod-noh-toh see vreh-meh.*)

730. He's an astronomy enthusiast.
Той е ентусиаст по астрономия.
(*Toy eh en-too-see-ahst poh ah-stroh-noh-mee-ya.*)

731. I've skydived twice.
Два пъти съм правил скок с парашут.
(*Dvah puh-tee sum prah-veel skohk s pah-rah-shoot.*)

732. She's a fitness trainer.
Тя е фитнес инструктор.
(*Tyah eh feet-nes in-struk-tor.*)

733. I love collecting vintage records.
Обичам да събирам винтидж плочи.
(*Oh-bee-cham dah suh-bee-ram veen-teej ploh-chee.*)

734. He's an experienced scuba diver.
Той е опитен водолаз.
(*Toy eh oh-pee-ten voh-doh-lahz.*)

735. He's a bookworm and a literature lover.
Той е книголюб и обичащ литературата.
(*Toy eh k-nee-goh-lyoob ee oh-bee-chatsh lee-teh-rah-too-rah-tah.*)

> **Fun Fact:** The Horo, a traditional Bulgarian folk dance, is a staple at weddings and celebrations.

Expressing Emotions and Sentiments

736. I feel overjoyed on my birthday.
Чувствам се изключително щастлив на рождения си ден.
(*Chuhv-stvahm seh eez-kloo-chee-tehl-noh shtah-stleev nah rohj-deh-nee-ya see den.*)

737. She's going through a tough time right now.
Тя преминава през труден период в момента.
(*Tyah preh-mee-nah-vah prehz troo-den peh-ree-od v mo-men-tah.*)

738. I'm thrilled about my upcoming vacation.
Вълнувам се много за предстоящата си почивка.
(*Vul-noo-vahm seh mnoh-goh zah prehd-stoy-ah-sh-tah see poh-cheev-kah.*)

739. He's heartbroken after the breakup.
Той е съсипан след раздялата.
(*Toy eh suh-see-pahn slehd raz-dya-lah-tah.*)

740. I'm absolutely ecstatic about the news.
Абсолютно съм въодушевен от новината.
(*Ab-soh-lyoot-noh soom vuh-oh-doo-sheh-vehn oht noh-vee-nah-tah.*)

741. She's feeling anxious before the big presentation.
Тя се чувства притеснена преди голямата презентация.
(*Tyah seh choov-stvah pree-tehs-neh-nah preh-dee goh-lya-mah-tah preh-zen-tah-tsee-yah.*)

742. I'm proud of my team's achievements.
Горд съм от постиженията на моя отбор.
(*Gohrd soom oht pohs-tee-zheh-nee-yah-tah nah moh-yah oht-bohr.*)

743. He's devastated by the loss.
Той е опустошен от загубата.
(*Toy eh oh-poo-stoh-shehn oht zah-goo-bah-tah.*)

744. I'm grateful for the support I received.
Благодарен съм за получената подкрепа.
(*Blah-goh-dah-rehn soom zah poh-loo-cheh-nah-tah pohd-kreh-pah.*)

745. She's experiencing a mix of emotions.
Тя изпитва смес от емоции.
(*Tyah eez-pee-tvah smehs oht eh-moh-tsee-ee.*)

746. I'm content with where I am in life.
Доволен съм от това, къде съм в живота си.
(*Doh-voh-lehn soom oht toh-vah, kuh-deh soom v zhi-voh-tah see.*)

747. He's overwhelmed by the workload.
Той е претоварен от работната натовареност.
(*Toy eh preh-toh-vah-ren oht rah-boht-nah-tah nah-toh-vah-reh-nost.*)

748. I'm in awe of the natural beauty here.
Възхитен съм от природната красота тук.
(*Vuhz-hee-tehn soom oht pree-rohd-nah-tah krah-soh-tah took.*)

> **Language Learning Tip:** Learn Bulgarian Songs by Heart - Singing can improve language skills.

749. She's relieved the exams are finally over.
Тя е облекчена, че изпитите най-накрая свършиха.
(*Tyah eh oh-bleh-cheh-nah, cheh eez-pee-tee-teh niy-nah-krah-yah svoor-shee-hah.*)

750. I'm excited about the new job opportunity.
Вълнувам се от новата възможност за работа.
(*Vul-noo-vahm seh oht noh-vah-tah vuhz-mohzh-nost zah rah-boh-tah.*)

Travel Story: During a sunset at Cape Kaliakra, a visitor whispered, "Залезът говори без думи" (The sunset speaks without words), capturing the beauty of the moment.

751. I'm nostalgic about my childhood.
Носталгичен съм по моето детство.
(Nos-tal-gee-chen soom po mo-eh-to deht-stvo.)

752. She's confused about her future.
Тя е объркана относно бъдещето си.
(Tyah eh ob-yoor-kah-nah oht-noh-sno buh-deh-sheh-toh see.)

753. I'm touched by the kindness of strangers.
Трогнат съм от добротата на непознатите.
(Trog-nat soom oht doh-broh-tah-tah nah neh-pohz-nah-tee-teh.)

754. He's envious of his friend's success.
Завижда на успеха на своя приятел.
(Zah-veezh-dah nah oos-peh-hah nah svo-yah pree-ya-tehl.)

755. I'm hopeful for a better tomorrow.
Надявам се за по-добро утре.
(Nah-dya-vam seh zah poh-doh-broh oo-treh.)

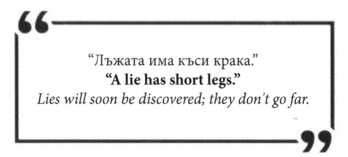

"Лъжата има къси крака."
"A lie has short legs."
Lies will soon be discovered; they don't go far.

Interactive Challenge: Family & Relationships
(Link each English word with their corresponding meaning in Bulgarian)

1) Family   Приятелство

2) Parents   Родители

3) Siblings   Осиновяване

4) Children   Братовчеди/Братовчедки

5) Grandparents   Брак

6) Spouse   Развод

7) Marriage   Любов

8) Love   Семейство

9) Friendship   Деца

10) Relatives   Съпруг/Съпруга

11) In-laws   Роднини

12) Divorce   Племенница

13) Adoption   Свекърви/Свекър

14) Cousins   Баби и дядовци

15) Niece   Братя и сестри

Correct Answers:

1. Family - Семейство
2. Parents - Родители
3. Siblings - Братя и сестри
4. Children - Деца
5. Grandparents - Баби и дядовци
6. Spouse - Съпруг/Съпруга
7. Marriage - Брак
8. Love - Любов
9. Friendship - Приятелство
10. Relatives - Роднини
11. In-laws - Свекърви/Свекър
12. Divorce - Развод
13. Adoption - Осиновяване
14. Cousins - Братовчеди/Братовчедки
15. Niece - Племенница

TECHNOLOGY & COMMUNICATION

- USING TECHNOLOGY-RELATED PHRASES -
- INTERNET ACCESS AND COMMUNICATION TOOLS -
- TROUBLESHOOTING TECHNICAL ISSUES -

Using Technology

756. I use my smartphone for various tasks.
      Използвам своя смартфон за различни задачи.
      (*Iz-polz-vam svo-ya smart-fon za raz-lich-ni za-da-chi.*)

757. The computer is an essential tool in my work.
      Компютърът е съществен инструмент в моята работа.
      (*Kom-pyu-tu-ruht eh su-shtes-tven in-stru-ment v mo-ya-ta ra-bo-ta.*)

758. I'm learning how to code and develop software.
      Уча се как да програмирам и разработвам софтуер.
      (*Oo-cha se kak da pro-gra-mi-ram i raz-ra-bot-vam soft-u-er.*)

759. My tablet helps me stay organized.
      Таблетът ми помага да остана организиран.
      (*Ta-ble-tuht mi po-ma-ga da os-ta-na or-ga-ni-ziran.*)

760. I enjoy exploring new apps and software.
      Харесва ми да изследвам нови приложения и софтуер.
      (*Ha-res-va mi da iz-sled-vam no-vi pri-lo-zhe-ni-ya i soft-u-er.*)

      Fun Fact: Bulgarians celebrate Baba Marta on March 1st by exchanging martenitsi, red and white adornments.

761. Smartwatches are becoming more popular.
      Умните часовници стават все по-популярни.
      (*Um-ni-te cha-sov-ni-tsi sta-vat vse po-po-pu-lyar-ni.*)

762. Virtual reality technology is fascinating.
Технологията на виртуалната реалност е фасцинираща.
(*Teh-no-lo-gi-ya-ta na vir-tu-al-na-ta re-al-nost eh fas-tsi-ni-ra-shta.*)

763. Artificial intelligence is changing industries.
Изкуственият интелект променя индустриите.
(*Iz-kus-tve-ni-yat in-te-lekt pro-me-nya in-dus-tri-i-te.*)

764. I like to customize my gadgets.
Харесвам да персонализирам моите устройства.
(*Ha-res-vam da per-so-na-li-zi-ram moi-te us-troi-stva.*)

765. E-books have replaced physical books for me.
Електронните книги заместиха хартиените за мен.
(*E-lek-tron-ni-te k-ni-gi za-mes-ti-ha har-ti-e-ni-te za men.*)

766. Social media platforms connect people worldwide.
Социалните медии платформи свързват хората по целия свят.
(*So-tsi-al-ni-te me-dii plat-for-mi svurz-vat ho-ra-ta po tse-li-ya svyat.*)

767. I'm a fan of wearable technology.
Фен съм на носимата технология.
(*Fen sum na no-si-ma-ta teh-no-lo-gi-ya.*)

768. The latest gadgets always catch my eye.
Най-новите гаджети винаги привличат вниманието ми.
(*Nai-no-vi-te gad-zhe-ti vi-na-gi pri-vli-chat vni-ma-nie-to mi.*)

769. My digital camera captures high-quality photos.
Моят цифров фотоапарат прави снимки високо качество.
(*Moyat tsi-frov fo-to-ah-pa-rat pra-vi snim-ki vi-so-ko ka-ches-tvo.*)

770. Home automation simplifies daily tasks.
Домашната автоматизация улеснява ежедневните задачи.
(*Do-mash-na-ta av-to-ma-ti-za-tsi-ya oo-les-nya-va e-zhe-dnev-ni-te za-da-chi.*)

771. I'm into 3D printing as a hobby.
3D печатът е моето хоби.
(*Tre-de pee-cha-tut e mo-e-to ho-bi.*)

772. Streaming services have revolutionized entertainment.
Стрийминг услугите преобразиха забавленията.
(*Streem-ing oos-loo-gi-te pre-o-bra-zi-ha za-bav-le-nya-ta.*)

773. The Internet of Things (IoT) is expanding.
Интернет на нещата (IoT) се разширява.
(*In-ter-net na neshta-ta se raz-shir-ya-va.*)

774. I'm into gaming, both console and PC.
Харесвам игри, както на конзола, така и на компютър.
(*Ha-res-vam ig-ri, kak-to na kon-zo-la, ta-ka i na kom-pyu-tar.*)

775. Wireless headphones make life more convenient.
Безжичните слушалки правят живота по-удобен.
(*Bez-zhi-chni-te sloo-shal-ki pra-vyat zhi-vo-ta po-oo-do-ben.*)

776. Cloud storage is essential for my work.
Облачното съхранение е съществено за моята работа.
(*Ob-lach-no-to sar-hra-ne-nie e susth-est-ve-no za moy-a-ta ra-bo-ta.*)

> **Travel Story:** At a lavender field near Kazanlak, a farmer explained, "Лавандулата е цветът на спокойствието" (Lavender is the color of tranquility), highlighting the calming effect of the landscape.

Internet Access and Communication Tools

777. I rely on high-speed internet for work.
Разчитам на бърз интернет за работа.
(*Raz-chi-tam na barz in-ter-net za ra-bo-ta.*)

778. Video conferencing is crucial for remote meetings.
Видеоконференциите са ключови за дистанционните срещи.
(*Vi-de-o-kon-fe-ren-tsi-i-te sa klyu-cho-vi za dis-tan-tsi-on-ni-te sreshti.*)

779. Social media helps me stay connected with friends.
Социалните медии ми помагат да остана във връзка с приятели.
(*So-tsi-al-ni-te me-di-i mi po-ma-gat da os-ta-na vav vrask-a s pri-ya-te-li.*)

780. Email is my primary mode of communication.
Имейлът е моят основен начин на комуникация.
(*I-mey-lut e moy-at os-no-ven na-chin na ko-mu-ni-ka-tsi-ya.*)

781. I use messaging apps to chat with family.
Използвам приложения за чат със семейството.
(*Iz-polz-vam pri-lo-zhe-ni-ya za chat sas se-mey-stvo-to.*)

782. Voice and video calls keep me in touch with loved ones.
Гласовите и видео разговори ме държат в контакт с близките.
(*Gla-so-vi-te i vi-de-o raz-go-vo-ri me dar-zhat v kon-takt s bli-zki-te.*)

783. Online forums are a great source of information.
Онлайн форумите са страхотен източник на информация.
(*On-layn fo-ru-mi-te sa stra-ho-ten iz-toch-nik na in-for-ma-tsi-ya.*)

784. I trust encrypted messaging services for privacy.
Доверявам се на криптирани услуги за съобщения заради поверителност.
(*Do-ve-rya-vam se na krip-ti-ra-ni oos-loo-gi za sa-ob-sche-ni-ya za-ra-di po-ve-ri-tel-nost.*)

785. Webinars are a valuable resource for learning.
Уебинарите са ценен ресурс за обучение.
(*Ue-bi-na-ri-te sa tse-nen re-surs za o-bu-che-ni-e.*)

> **Idiomatic Expression:** "Режа си носа." -
> Meaning: "To spite oneself."
> (Literal translation: "I cut my nose.")

786. VPNs enhance online security and privacy.
VPN-ите повишават онлайн сигурността и поверителността.
(*Vee-Pee-En-i-te po-vi-sha-vat on-layn si-gur-nost-ta i po-ve-ri-tel-nost-ta.*)

787. Cloud-based collaboration tools are essential for teamwork.
Облачните инструменти за сътрудничество са съществени за екипната работа.
(Ob-lach-ni-te in-stru-men-ti za sa-trod-ni-ches-tvo sa sushtest-ve-ni za e-kip-na-ta ra-bo-ta.)

788. I prefer using a wireless router at home.
Предпочитам да използвам безжичен рутер у дома.
(Preh-dpo-chi-tam da iz-polz-vam bez-zhi-chen ru-ter u do-ma.)

789. Online banking simplifies financial transactions.
Онлайн банкирането улеснява финансовите трансакции.
(On-layn ban-ki-ra-ne-to oo-les-nya-va fi-nan-so-vi-te tran-sak-tsi-i.)

> **Fun Fact:** Bulgaria hosts various folklore festivals showcasing traditional music, dance, and costumes.

790. VoIP services are cost-effective for international calls.
VoIP услугите са икономични за международни разговори.
(VoyP oos-loo-gi-te sa i-ko-no-mich-ni za mezhdoo-na-rod-ni raz-go-vo-ri.)

791. I enjoy online shopping for convenience.
Харесвам онлайн пазаруването заради удобството.
(Ha-re-svam on-layn pa-za-ru-va-ne-to za-ra-di oo-dob-stvo-to.)

792. Social networking sites connect people globally.
Социалните мрежи свързват хората по целия свят.
(So-tsi-al-ni-te mre-zhi svarz-vat ho-ra-ta po tse-li-ya svyat.)

793. E-commerce platforms offer a wide variety of products.
E-commerce платформите предлагат широк асортимент продукти.
(*E-commerce plat-for-mi-te pred-la-gat shi-rok a-sor-ti-ment pro-duk-ti.*)

> **Idiomatic Expression:** "Вадя ти акъла." -
> Meaning: "To lecture or preach to someone."
> (Literal translation: "I take out your mind.")

794. Mobile banking apps make managing finances easy.
Мобилните банкови приложения улесняват управлението на финансите.
(*Mo-bil-ni-te ban-ko-vi pri-lo-zhe-ni-ya u-les-nya-vat up-ra-vle-nie-to na fi-nan-si-te.*)

795. I'm active on professional networking sites.
Активен съм в професионалните мрежи за нетуъркинг.
(*Ak-ti-ven sam v pro-fe-si-o-nal-ni-te mre-zhi za ne-tur-kin-g.*)

796. Virtual private networks protect my online identity.
Виртуалните частни мрежи защитават моята онлайн идентичност.
(*Vir-tu-al-ni-te chas-tni mre-zhi zash-ti-ta-vat mo-ya-ta on-layn i-den-tich-nost.*)

797. Instant messaging apps are great for quick chats.
Приложенията за моментални съобщения са страхотни за бързи разговори.
(*Pri-lo-zhe-ni-ya-ta za mo-men-tal-ni sa-ob-sche-ni-ya sa stra-hot-ni za bur-zi raz-go-vo-ri.*)

> **Cultural Insight:** Bulgarians take great pride in their language, which is the first Slavic language to be written and has a significant historical impact on Slavic culture.

Troubleshooting Technical Issues

798. My computer is running slow; I need to fix it.
Компютърът ми работи бавно; трябва да го оправя.
(Kom-pyu-tur-at mi ra-bo-ti bav-no; tryab-va da go o-pra-vya.)

799. I'm experiencing network connectivity problems.
Имам проблеми с връзката с мрежата.
(I-mam prob-le-mi s vrus-kata s mre-zha-ta.)

800. The printer isn't responding to my print commands.
Принтерът не реагира на моите команди за печат.
(Prin-te-rat ne re-a-gi-ra na moi-te ko-man-di za pe-chat.)

> **Fun Fact:** Bulgaria hosts numerous cultural festivals, including the famous Rose Festival in Kazanlak.

801. My smartphone keeps freezing; it's frustrating.
Смартфонът ми постоянно замръзва; това е разочароващо.
(Smart-fo-nat mi pos-to-yan-no zam-raz-va; to-va e ra-zo-cha-ro-vashto.)

802. The Wi-Fi signal in my house is weak.
Wi-Fi сигналът в моят дом е слаб.
(Vee-Fee sig-na-lat v mo-yat dom e slab.)

803. I can't access certain websites; it's a concern.
Не мога да достъпя някои уебсайтове; това е притеснително.
(Ne mo-ga da dos-tup-ya nyakoi ueb-say-to-ve; to-va e pri-tes-ni-tel-no.)

804. My laptop battery drains quickly; I need a solution.
Батерията на лаптопа ми се изтощава бързо; трябва ми решение.
(*Ba-te-ri-ya-ta na lap-to-pa mi se iz-tosh-ta-va bur-zo; tryab-va mi re-she-nie.*)

805. There's a software update available for my device.
Има налична софтуерна актуализация за моето устройство.
(*Ee-ma na-lich-na sof-tu-er-na ak-tu-a-li-za-tsi-ya za mo-e-to u-stroy-stvo.*)

806. My email account got locked; I need to recover it.
Имейл акаунтът ми беше заключен; трябва да го възстановя.
(*Ee-mayl a-kown-tut mi be-she za-klyu-chen; tryab-va da go vuz-sta-nov-ya.*)

> **Fun Fact:** Traditional Bulgarian folk costumes are colorful and vary significantly from region to region.

807. The screen on my tablet is cracked; I'm upset.
Екранът на таблета ми е счупен; много съм разстроен.
(*Ek-ran-ut na ta-ble-ta mi e schu-pen; mno-go sum raz-stro-en.*)

808. My webcam isn't working during video calls.
Уеб камерата ми не работи по време на видео разговори.
(*U-eb ka-me-ra-ta mi ne ra-bo-ti po vre-me na vi-de-o raz-go-vo-ri.*)

809. My phone's storage is almost full; I need to clear it.
Паметта на телефона ми е почти пълна; трябва да я изчистя.
(*Pa-met-ta na te-le-fo-na mi e poch-ti pul-na; tryab-va da ya iz-chis-tya.*)

810. I accidentally deleted important files; I need help.
Случайно изтрих важни файлове; нуждая се от помощ.
(*Slu-chay-no iz-trih vazh-ni fay-lo-ve; noozh-daya se ot pom-osht.*)

> **Fun Fact:** Bulgarian is unique among Slavic languages for having eliminated case declensions.

811. My smart home devices are not responding.
Моите умни домашни устройства не реагират.
(*Moi-te um-ni do-mash-ni u-stroy-stva ne re-a-gi-rat.*)

812. The GPS on my navigation app is inaccurate.
GPS-ът в моето навигационно приложение е неточен.
(*Je-Pe-Es-at v mo-e-to na-vi-ga-tsi-on-no pri-lo-zhe-nie e ne-to-chen.*)

813. My antivirus software detected a threat; I'm worried.
Антивирусният ми софтуер откри заплаха; притеснен съм.
(*An-ti-vi-rus-ni-yat mi sof-tu-er ot-kri zap-lah-a; pri-tes-nen sum.*)

814. The touchscreen on my device is unresponsive.
Сензорният екран на устройството ми не реагира.
(*Sen-zor-ni-yat ek-ran na u-stroy-stvo-to mi ne re-a-gi-ra.*)

815. My gaming console is displaying error messages.
Игралната ми конзола показва грешки.
(*I-gral-na-ta mi kon-zo-la po-kaz-va gre-shki.*)

> **Fun Fact:** Unlike most Slavic languages, Bulgarian often reduces unstressed vowels.

816.   I'm locked out of my social media account.
        Изключен съм от моя социален медиен акаунт.
        (Iz-kloo-chen sum ot mo-ya so-tsi-a-len me-di-en a-kownt.)

817.   The sound on my computer is distorted.
        Звукът на моя компютър е изкривен.
        (Zvoo-kut na mo-ya kom-pyoo-tur e iz-kri-ven.)

818.   My email attachments won't open; it's frustrating.
        **Прикачените файлове към имейла ми не се отварят; това
        е разочароващо.**
        *(Pri-ka-che-ni-te fay-lo-ve kam i-mey-la mi ne se ot-va-ryat; to-va
        e ra-zo-cha-ro-va-shto.)*

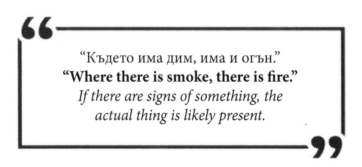

"Където има дим, има и огън."
"Where there is smoke, there is fire."
*If there are signs of something, the
actual thing is likely present.*

Cross Word Puzzle: Technology & Communication
(Provide the English translation for the following Bulgarian words)

Down

2. - БАТЕРИЯ
5. - КРИПТОЛОГИЯ
7. - ВХОД
8. - БРАУЗЪР
10. - ОБЛАК
11. - ИНТЕРНЕТ
13. - РУТЕР
15. - КОМПЮТЪР

Across

1. - УЕБ КАМЕРА
3. - ДАННИ
4. - ЕКРАН
6. - КЛАВИАТУРА
9. - ПРИЛОЖЕНИЯ
12. - ПРИНТЕР
14. - ЗАРЯДНО
16. - МРЕЖА

185

Correct Answers:

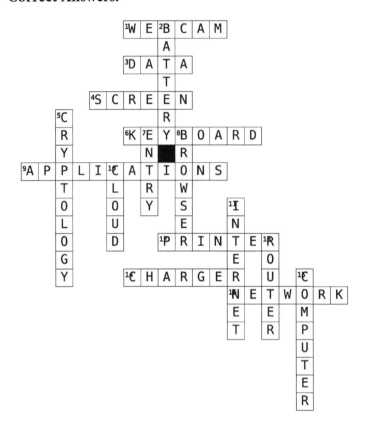

SPORTS & RECREATION

- DISCUSSING SPORTS, GAMES, & OUTDOOR ACTIVITIES -
- PARTICIPATING IN RECREATIONAL ACTIVITIES -
- EXPRESSING ENTHUSUASM OR FRUSTRATION -

Sports, Games, & Outdoor Activities

819. I love playing soccer with my friends.
Обичам да играя футбол с приятелите си.
(Oh-bee-cham da ee-graya foot-bol s pree-ya-te-lee-te si.)

820. Basketball is a fast-paced and exciting sport.
Баскетболът е бърз и вълнуващ спорт.
(Bas-ket-bo-lut e burz ee vul-noo-vash sport.)

821. Let's go for a hike in the mountains this weekend.
Нека отидем на планински преход този уикенд.
(Ne-ka o-tee-dem na pla-neen-ski pre-hod to-zi wee-kend.)

822. Playing chess helps improve my strategic thinking.
Играта на шах подобрява моята стратегическа мисъл.
(Ee-gra-ta na shah po-do-brya-va mo-ya-ta stra-te-gee-ska mee-sul.)

823. I'm a fan of tennis; it requires a lot of skill.
Фен съм на тениса; изисква много умения.
(Fen sum na te-nee-sa; ee-seesk-va mnogo oo-me-nee-ya.)

824. Are you up for a game of volleyball at the beach?
Желаете ли игра на волейбол на плажа?
(Zhe-lie-te li ee-gra na vo-lei-bol na plazh-a?)

825. Let's organize a game of ultimate frisbee.
Да организираме игра на ultimate frisbee.
(Da or-ga-nee-ze-ra-me ee-gra na ultimate frisbee.)

826. Baseball games are a great way to spend the afternoon.
Бейзболните игри са чудесен начин да прекарате следобеда.
(*Beyz-bol-ni-te ee-gri sa choo-de-sen na-cheen da pre-ka-ra-te sle-do-bed-a.*)

827. Camping in the wilderness is so peaceful.
Къмпингът в дивата природа е толкова спокоен.
(*Kum-ping-ut v dee-va-ta pree-ro-da e tol-ko-va spo-ko-en.*)

828. I enjoy swimming in the local pool.
Обичам да плувам в местния басейн.
(*Oh-bee-cham da ploo-vam v mes-tni-ya ba-seyn.*)

829. I'm learning to play the guitar in my free time.
Уча се да свиря на китара в свободното си време.
(*Oo-cha se da svi-rya na ki-ta-ra v svo-bo-dno-to si vre-me.*)

830. Skiing in the winter is an exhilarating experience.
Ският през зимата е вълнуващо преживяване.
(*Ski-yat prez zee-ma-ta e vul-noo-va-shto prezhi-vya-va-ne.*)

831. Going fishing by the lake is so relaxing.
Риболовът край езерото е толкова релаксиращ.
(*Ree-bo-lo-vut kray e-ze-ro-to e tol-ko-va re-lak-see-rasht.*)

832. We should have a board game night with friends.
Трябва да организираме вечер на настолни игри с приятели.
(*Tryab-va da or-ga-nee-ze-ra-me ve-cher na nas-tol-ni ee-gri s pree-ya-te-li.*)

Travel Story: In the bustling Central Market Hall in Sofia, a vendor said, "Всеки аромат разказва история" (Every scent tells a story), emphasizing the sensory experience of Bulgarian markets.

833. Martial arts training keeps me fit and disciplined.
Тренировките по бойни изкуства ме поддържат във форма и дисциплинирани.
(*Tre-nee-rov-ki-te po boi-ni iz-kus-tva me pod-dur-zhat vuv for-ma i dis-tsee-plee-nee-ra-nee.*)

834. I'm a member of a local running club.
Член съм на местен бегачески клуб.
(*Chlen sum na mes-ten be-ga-che-ski klub.*)

835. Playing golf is a great way to unwind.
Играта на голф е страхотен начин да се отпусна.
(*Ee-gra-ta na golf e stra-ho-ten na-chin da se ot-pus-na.*)

> **Idiomatic Expression:** "Гледам през пръсти." -
> Meaning: "To overlook or ignore."
> (Literal translation: "I look through fingers.")

836. Yoga classes help me stay flexible and calm.
Йога класовете ми помагат да остана гъвкав и спокоен.
(*Yo-ga klas-o-ve-te mi po-ma-gat da os-ta-na guv-kav i spo-ko-en.*)

837. I can't wait to go snowboarding this season.
Не мога да дочакам да отида на сноуборд този сезон.
(*Ne mo-ga da do-cha-kam da o-tee-da na sno-u-bord to-zi se-zon.*)

838. Going kayaking down the river is an adventure.
Каякингът по реката е приключение.
(*Ka-ya-kin-gut po re-ka-ta e pri-klyu-che-nie.*)

839. Let's organize a picnic in the park.
Да организираме пикник в парка.
(*Da or-ga-nee-ze-ra-me pik-nik v par-ka.*)

Participating in Recreational Activities

840. I enjoy painting landscapes as a hobby.
Хобито ми е да рисувам пейзажи.
(Ho-bi-to mi e da ri-su-vam pei-za-zhi.)

841. Gardening is a therapeutic way to spend my weekends.
Градинарството е терапевтичен начин да прекарвам уикендите си.
(Gra-di-nar-stvo-to e te-ra-pee-vti-chen na-chin da pre-kar-vam u-i-ken-di-te si.)

842. Playing the piano is my favorite pastime.
Да свиря на пиано е любимото ми занимание.
(Da svi-rya na pi-a-no e lyu-bi-mo-to mi za-ni-ma-nie.)

843. Reading books helps me escape into different worlds.
Четенето на книги ми помага да избягам в различни светове.
(Che-te-ne-to na k-ni-gi mi po-ma-ga da iz-byag-am v raz-lich-ni sve-to-ve.)

844. I'm a regular at the local dance classes.
Редовно посещавам местните танцови курсове.
(Re-dov-no po-se-schav-am mes-tni-te tan-tso-vi kur-so-ve.)

845. Woodworking is a skill I've been honing.
Дърводелството е умение, което развивам.
(Dur-vo-del-stvo-to e oo-me-nie, ko-e-to raz-vi-vam.)

> **Idiomatic Expression:** "Не ми се занимава." -
> Meaning: "I don't feel like dealing with it."
> (Literal translation: "I don't want to deal with it.")

846. I find solace in birdwatching at the nature reserve.
Намирам утеха в наблюдаването на птици в природен резерват.
(*Na-mee-ram oo-te-ha v nab-lyu-da-va-ne-to na pti-tsi v pri-ro-den re-zer-vat.*)

847. Meditation and mindfulness keep me centered.
Медитацията и осъзнатостта ме поддържат съсредоточен.
(*Me-di-ta-tsi-ya-ta i o-suz-na-tost-ta me pod-dur-jat sus-re-do-to-chen.*)

848. I've taken up photography to capture moments.
Започнах да се занимавам с фотография, за да запечатам моментите.
(*Za-poch-nah da se za-ni-ma-vam s fo-to-gra-fi-ya, za da za-pe-chat-am mo-men-ti-te.*)

849. Going to the gym is part of my daily routine.
Посещението на фитнеса е част от моето ежедневие.
(*Po-se-she-ni-e-to na fit-ne-sa e chast ot mo-e-to e-zhe-dnev-i-e.*)

850. Cooking new recipes is a creative outlet for me.
Готвенето на нови рецепти е моят творчески израз.
(*Got-ve-ne-to na no-vi re-tsep-ti e mo-yat tvor-ches-ki iz-raz.*)

851. Building model airplanes is a fascinating hobby.
Сглобяването на модели самолети е завладяващо хоби.
(*Sglo-byav-a-ne-to na mo-de-li sa-mo-le-ti e zav-la-dya-vashto ho-bi.*)

852. I love attending art exhibitions and galleries.
Обичам да посещавам изложби на изкуство и галерии.
(*O-bi-cham da po-se-shta-vam iz-lozh-bi na iz-kus-tvo i ga-le-rii.*)

853. Collecting rare stamps has been a lifelong passion.
Събирането на редки пощенски марки е моя страст за цял живот.
(*Sab-i-ra-ne-to na red-ki posh-ten-ski mar-ki e mo-ya strast za tsyal zhi-vot.*)

854. I'm part of a community theater group.
Част съм от театрална общностна група.
(*Chast sum ot te-a-tral-na obsh-nost-na gru-pa.*)

855. Birdwatching helps me connect with nature.
Наблюдаването на птици ми помага да се свържа с природата.
(*Nab-lyu-da-va-ne-to na pti-tsi mi po-ma-ga da se svur-jha s pri-ro-da-ta.*)

856. I'm an avid cyclist and explore new trails.
Страстен колоездач съм и изследвам нови пътеки.
(*Stras-ten ko-lo-ez-dach sum i iz-sled-vam no-vi puh-te-ki.*)

857. Pottery classes allow me to express myself.
Часовете по керамика ми позволяват да се изразя.
(*Chas-o-ve-te po ke-ra-mi-ka mi poz-vo-lya-vat da se iz-ra-zya.*)

858. Playing board games with family is a tradition.
Играта на настолни игри със семейството е традиция.
(*Ig-ra-ta na nas-tol-ni ig-ri sus se-mey-stvo-to e tra-di-tsi-ya.*)

859. I'm practicing mindfulness through meditation.
Практикувам осъзнатост чрез медитация.
(*Pra-k-ti-ku-vam o-suz-na-tost chrez me-di-ta-tsi-ya.*)

860. I enjoy long walks in the park with my dog.
Обичам да ходя на дълги разходки в парка с моето куче.
(*O-bi-cham da ho-dya na dŭl-gi raz-hod-ki v par-ka s mo-e-to ku-che.*)

> **Travel Story:** At a traditional kukeri festival, a masked performer stated, "Маските прогонват злите духове" (The masks chase away evil spirits), explaining the purpose of the ancient ritual.

Expressing Enthusiasm or Frustration

861. I'm thrilled we won the championship!
Много съм развълнуван, че спечелихме шампионата!
(*Mno-go sŭm raz-vŭl-nu-van, che spe-che-lih-me sham-pi-o-na-ta!*)

862. Scoring that goal felt amazing.
Отбелязването на този гол беше невероятно.
(*Ot-be-lyaz-va-ne-to na to-zi gol be-she ne-ve-ro-yat-no.*)

863. It's so frustrating when we lose a game.
Много е фрустриращо, когато загубим мач.
(*Mno-go e frus-tri-ra-shto, ko-ga-to za-gu-bim mach.*)

864. I can't wait to play again next week.
Не мога да дочакам да играя отново следващата седмица.
(*Ne mo-ga da do-cha-kam da ig-ra-ya ot-no-vo sled-va-shta-ta se-dmi-tsa.*)

> **Fun Fact:** After roses, lavender is another significant essential oil crop in Bulgaria.

865. Our team's performance was outstanding.
Изпълнението на нашия отбор беше изключително.
(*Iz-pŭl-ne-nie-to na na-shi-ya ot-bor be-she iz-klyu-chi-tel-no.*)

866. We need to practice more; we keep losing.
Трябва да тренираме повече; непрекъснато губим.
(*Tryab-va da tre-ni-ra-me po-ve-che; ne-pre-kŭs-na-to gu-bim.*)

867. I'm over the moon about our victory!
Изключително съм щастлив от нашата победа!
(*Iz-klyu-chi-tel-no sŭm shchas-tliv ot na-sha-ta po-be-da!*)

> **Language Learning Tip:** Take Notes by Hand - It helps better with memory retention.

868. I'm an avid cyclist and explore new trails.
Страстен колоездач съм и изследвам нови пътеки.
(*Stras-ten ko-lo-ez-dach sŭm i iz-sled-vam no-vi pŭ-te-ki.*)

869. The referee's decision was unfair.
Решението на съдията беше несправедливо.
(*Re-she-nie-to na sŭ-di-ya-ta be-she ne-spra-ved-li-vo.*)

870. We've been on a winning streak lately.
Наскоро сме на печеливша серия.
(*Nas-ko-ro sme na pe-che-liv-sha se-ri-ya.*)

871. I'm disappointed in our team's performance.
Разочарован съм от представянето на нашия отбор.
(*Ra-zo-cha-ro-van sŭm ot pred-stav-ya-ne-to na na-shi-ya ot-bor.*)

872. The adrenaline rush during the race was incredible.
Адреналиновият прилив по време на състезанието беше невероятен.
(*Ad-reh-na-lee-no-vi-yat pri-liv po vre-me na sŭ-ste-za-nie-to be-she ne-ve-ro-ya-ten.*)

873. We need to step up our game to compete.
Трябва да подобрим играта си, за да се състезаваме.
(*Tryab-va da po-do-b-rim ig-ra-ta si, za da se sŭ-ste-za-va-me.*)

874. Winning the tournament was a dream come true.
Победата в турнира беше осъществена мечта.
(*Po-be-da-ta v tur-ni-ra be-she o-sŭ-shtest-ve-na mech-ta.*)

875. I was so close to scoring a goal.
Бях толкова близо до отбелязване на гол.
(*Byah tol-ko-va bli-zo do ot-be-lyaz-va-ne na gol.*)

876. We should celebrate our recent win.
Трябва да отпразнуваме нашата скорошна победа.
(*Tryab-va da ot-praz-nu-va-me na-sha-ta sko-rosh-na po-be-da.*)

877. Losing by a narrow margin is frustrating.
Губенето с малка разлика е фрустриращо.
(*Gu-be-ne-to s mal-ka raz-li-ka e frus-tri-ra-shto.*)

878. Let's train harder to improve our skills.
Нека тренираме по-усилено, за да подобрим уменията си.
(*Ne-ka tre-ni-ra-me po-u-si-le-no, za da po-do-brim u-me-ni-ya-ta si.*)

879.   The match was intense from start to finish.
       Мачът беше интензивен от началото до края.
       (Ma-chŭt be-she in-ten-zi-ven ot na-cha-lo-to do kra-ya.)

880.   I'm proud of our team's sportsmanship.
       Гордея се със спортсменството на нашия отбор.
       (Gor-de-ya se sŭs spor-ts-men-stvo-to na na-shi-ya ot-bor.)

881.   We've faced tough competition this season.
       Този сезон се сблъскахме с тежка конкуренция.
       (To-zi se-zon se sblŭ-ska-hme s tezh-ka kon-ku-ren-tsi-ya.)

882.   I'm determined to give it my all in the next game.
       Решен съм да дам всичко от себе си в следващата игра.
       *(Re-shen sŭm da dam v-sich-ko ot se-be si v sled-va-shcha-ta
       ig-ra.)*

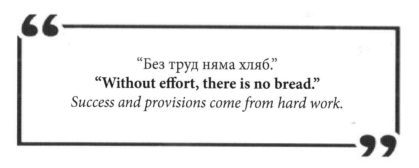

"Без труд няма хляб."
"Without effort, there is no bread."
Success and provisions come from hard work.

Mini Lesson:
Basic Grammar Principles in Bulgarian #3

Introduction:

As we continue our exploration of Bulgarian, a South Slavic language, understanding its complex grammar is key to mastering both spoken and written forms. This lesson will build upon our previous discussions, diving into more intricate aspects of Bulgarian grammar that are essential for nuanced communication.

1. Sentence Structure:

Bulgarian typically follows a Subject-Verb-Object (SVO) sentence structure, but due to its flexible syntax, variations are common depending on emphasis and context.

- *Аз чета книга. (I read a book.)*
- *Книга чета аз. (A book is what I am reading - emphasis on the book.)*

2. Clitics:

Clitics are special words in Bulgarian that are phonologically dependent on neighboring words and often serve grammatical functions.

- *Дай ми го. (Give it to me. - "ми" and "го" are clitics.)*

3. Participles:

Participles are verbal adjectives or adverbs in Bulgarian, used to form complex tenses, passive voices, or as adjectives.

- *Четящият мъж (The man who is reading)*
- *Писана книга (A written book)*

4. Conjunctions:

Bulgarian uses conjunctions to connect clauses or words, with common ones being "и" (and), "но" (but), and "или" (or).

- *Той идва и тя отива. (He comes and she goes.)*

5. Numerals and Quantifiers:

Bulgarian distinguishes between cardinal, ordinal, and quantifying numerals.

- *Един, два, три (one, two, three - cardinal)*
- *Първи, втори, трети (first, second, third - ordinal)*
- *Много книги (many books - quantifier)*

6. Subjunctive and Conditional Moods:

The subjunctive and conditional moods in Bulgarian express wishes, hypotheses, or conditions.

- *Да отида там (To go there - subjunctive)*
- *Бих отишъл, ако можех. (I would go if I could - conditional)*

7. Compound Sentences:

Bulgarian forms compound sentences using coordinating or subordinating conjunctions.

- *Това е моята книга. (This is my book.)*

8. Expressing Possession:

Possession in Bulgarian is typically expressed using possessive pronouns or the dative case.

- *Искам да отида, но нямам време. (I want to go, but I don't have time.)*
- *Книгата е на Иван. (The book is Ivan's - using dative.)*

Conclusion:

This deeper dive into Bulgarian grammar reveals the language's richness and complexity. Understanding these concepts will greatly aid your fluency. Keep practicing, and remember that immersion and regular use are key to mastering Bulgarian. Успех! (Good luck!)

TRANSPORT & DIRECTIONS

- ASKING FOR AND GIVING DIRECTIONS -
- USING TRANSPORTATION-RELATED PHRASES -

Asking for and Giving Directions

883.   Can you tell me how to get to the nearest subway station?
Можете ли да ми кажете как да стигна до най-близката метростанция?
(Mozhe-teh lee da mee kah-zheh-teh kak da stig-na do nai-bli-za-ta me-tro-stan-tsi-ya?)

884.   Excuse me, where's the bus stop for Route 25?
Извинете, къде е спирката за автобус номер 25?
(Iz-vi-ne-teh, kŭ-deh eh spi-rka-ta za av-to-bus no-mer dvah-dye-set i peht?)

885.   Could you give me directions to the city center?
Можете ли да ми дадете указания до центъра на града?
(Mozhe-teh lee da mee dah-deh-teh oo-ka-za-ni-ya do tsehn-tŭ-ra na gra-da?)

886.   I'm looking for a good place to eat around here. Any recommendations?
Търся хубаво място за хранене наоколо. Имате ли препоръки?
(Tŭr-sya hu-ba-vo myas-to za hra-ne-ne na-o-ko-lo. I-ma-teh lee pre-po-rŭ-ki?)

887.   Which way is the nearest pharmacy?
Коя е посоката към най-близката аптека?
(Ko-ya eh po-so-ka-ta kŭm nai-bli-za-ka-ta ap-te-ka?)

888.   How do I get to the airport from here?
Как да стигна до летището оттук?
(Kak da stig-na do le-ti-shche-to ott-tuk?)

889. Can you point me to the nearest ATM?
Можете ли да ми посочите къде е най-близкият банкомат?
(*Mozhe-teh lee da mee po-so-chee-teh kŭ-deh eh nai-bli-zki-yat banko-mat?*)

890. I'm lost. Can you help me find my way back to the hotel?
Изгубил съм се. Можете ли да ми помогнете да се върна обратно в хотела?
(*Iz-gu-bil sŭm seh. Mozhe-teh lee da mee po-mog-ne-teh da seh vŭr-na ob-rat-no v ho-te-la?*)

891. Where's the closest gas station?
Къде е най-близката бензиностанция?
(*Kŭ-deh eh nai-bli-za-ka-ta ben-zi-no-stan-tsi-ya?*)

892. Is there a map of the city available?
Има ли налична карта на града?
(*I-ma lee na-lich-na kar-ta na gra-da?*)

893. How far is it to the train station from here?
Колко е далеч до гарата оттук?
(*Kol-ko eh da-lech do ga-ra-ta ott-tuk?*)

894. Which exit should I take to reach the shopping mall?
Кой изход трябва да взема, за да стигна до търговския център?
(*Koi iz-hod tryab-va da vze-ma, za da stig-na do tŭr-go-vski-ya tsehn-tŭr?*)

895. Where can I find a taxi stand around here?
Къде мога да намеря таксиметрова спирка наоколо?
(*Kŭ-deh mo-ga da na-me-rya tak-si-me-tro-va spi-rka na-o-ko-lo?*)

896. Can you direct me to the main tourist attractions?
Можете ли да ме насочите към основните туристически атракции?
(*Mozhete li da me nasochite kŭm osnovnite turisticheski atraktsii?*)

> **Fun Fact:** The Belogradchik Rocks are a group of bizarrely shaped sandstone formations.

897. I need to go to the hospital. Can you provide directions?
Трябва да отида в болницата. Можете ли да ми дадете указания?
(*Tryabva da otida v bolnitsata. Mozhete li da mi dadete ukazaniya?*)

898. Is there a park nearby where I can go for a walk?
Има ли наблизо парк, къдетo мога да се разходя?
(*Ima li nablizo park, kŭdeto moga da se razhodya?*)

899. Which street should I take to reach the museum?
По коя улица да тръгна, за да стигна до музея?
(*Po koya ulitsa da trŭgna, za da stigna do muzeya?*)

900. How do I get to the concert venue?
Как да стигна до концертната зала?
(*Kak da stigna do kontsertnata zala?*)

901. Can you guide me to the nearest public restroom?
Можете ли да ме насочите към най-близката обществена тоалетна?
(*Mozhete li da me nasochite kŭm nai-blizkata obshtestvena toaletna?*)

902. Where's the best place to catch a cab in this area?
Къде е най-доброто място да хвана такси в този район?
(*Kŭde e nai-dobroto myasto da hvana taksi v tozi rayon?*)

Buying Tickets

903. I'd like to buy a one-way ticket to downtown, please.
Искам да купя еднопосочен билет за центъра, моля.
(*Iskam da kupya ednoposochen bilet za tsentŭra, molya.*)

904. How much is a round-trip ticket to the airport?
Колко струва двупосочен билет до летището?
(*Kolko struva dvuposochen bilet do letishteto?*)

905. Do you accept credit cards for ticket purchases?
Приемате ли кредитни карти за покупка на билети?
(*Priemate li kreditni karti za pokupka na bileti?*)

906. Can I get a student discount on this train ticket?
Мога ли да получа студентска отстъпка за този влаков билет?
(*Moga li da polucha studentska otstŭpka za tozi vlakov bilet?*)

907. Is there a family pass available for the bus?
Има ли семеен абонамент за автобуса?
(*Ima li semeen abonament za avtobusa?*)

> **Fun Fact:** Bulgaria has a strong tradition in weightlifting, with numerous Olympic medals.

908. What's the fare for a child on the subway?
    Каква е таксата за дете в метрото?
    (*Kakva e taksata za dete v metroto?*)

909. Are there any senior citizen discounts for tram tickets?
    Има ли отстъпки за възрастни хора за билети за трамвай?
    (*Ima li otstapki za vazrastni hora za bileti za tramvai?*)

910. Do I need to make a reservation for the express train?
    Трябва ли да направя резервация за експресния влак?
    (*Tryabva li da napravya rezervatsiya za ekspresniya vlak?*)

911. Can I upgrade to first class on this flight?
    Мога ли да премина в първа класа на този полет?
    (*Moga li da premina v parva klasa na tozi polet?*)

912. Are there any extra fees for luggage on this bus?
    Има ли допълнителни такси за багаж в този автобус?
    (*Ima li dopalnitelni taksi za bagazh v tozi avtobus?*)

913. I'd like to book a sleeper car for the overnight train.
    Искам да резервирам спален вагон за нощния влак.
    (*Iskam da rezerviram spalen vagon za noshtniya vlak.*)

914. What's the schedule for the next ferry to the island?
    Какъв е графикът за следващия ферибот до острова?
    (*Kakav e grafikat za sledvashtiya feribot do ostrova?*)

915. Are there any available seats on the evening bus to the beach?
Има ли свободни места на вечерния автобус за плажа?
(*Ima li svobodni mesta na vecherniya avtobus za plazha?*)

916. Can I pay for my metro ticket with a mobile app?
Мога ли да платя билета за метрото с мобилно приложение?
(*Moga li da platya bileta za metroto s mobilno prilozhenie?*)

917. Is there a discount for purchasing tickets online?
Има ли отстъпка при покупка на билети онлайн?
(*Ima li otstapka pri pokupka na bileti onlain?*)

918. How much is the parking fee at the train station?
Колко е таксата за паркиране на гарата?
(*Kolko e taksata za parkirane na garata?*)

919. I'd like to reserve two seats for the next shuttle bus.
Искам да резервирам две места за следващия шатъл автобус.
(*Iskam da rezerviram dve mesta za sledvashtiya shatal avtobus.*)

920. Do I need to validate my ticket before boarding the tram?
Трябва ли да валидирам билета си преди да се кача на трамвая?
(*Tryabva li da validiram bileta si predi da se kacha na tramvaya?*)

921. Can I buy a monthly pass for the subway?
Мога ли да купя месечен абонамент за метрото?
(*Moga li da kupya mesetschen abonament za metroto?*)

922. Are there any group rates for the boat tour?
Има ли групови тарифи за обиколката с лодка?
(*Ima li groo-poh-vi tah-ree-fi za oh-bee-kohl-ka-ta s lohd-ka?*)

> **Travel Story:** On a boat ride along the Danube, a sailor mused, "Реката води истории" (The river carries stories), referring to the river's historical significance.

Arranging Travel

923. I need to book a flight to Paris for next week.
Трябва да резервирам полет за Париж за следващата седмица.
(*Tryab-va da reh-zer-vee-ram po-let za Pa-reezh za sled-va-sha-ta sed-mee-tsa.*)

924. What's the earliest departure time for the high-speed train?
Какъв е най-ранният час на тръгване на бързия влак?
(*Ka-kuv e nai-ran-nee-yat chas na trug-va-ne na bur-zi-ya vlak?*)

925. Can I change my bus ticket to a later time?
Мога ли да променя билета си за автобус за по-късен час?
(*Mo-ga li da pro-me-nya bee-le-ta si za av-to-boos za po-kus-en chas?*)

926. I'd like to rent a car for a week.
Искам да наема кола за една седмица.
(*Ee-skam da na-e-ma ko-la za ed-na sed-mee-tsa.*)

927. Is there a direct flight to New York from here?
Има ли директен полет до Ню Йорк оттук?
(*Ee-ma li dee-rek-ten po-let do Nyu York ot-took?*)

928. I need to cancel my reservation for the cruise.
Трябва да анулирам резервацията си за круиза.
(*Tryab-va da a-noo-lee-ram reh-zer-va-tsi-ya-ta si za kroo-ee-za.*)

929. Can you help me find a reliable taxi service for airport transfers?
Можете ли да ми помогнете да намеря надеждна таксиметрова услуга за трансфери до летището?
(*Mo-zhe-te li da mi po-mog-ne-te da na-me-rya na-dezh-da tak-see-me-tro-va oo-sloo-ga za trans-fe-ree do le-teesh-te-to?*)

930. I'm interested in a guided tour of the city. How can I arrange that?
Интересувам се от водена обиколка на града. Как мога да организирам това?
(*Een-teh-re-soo-vam se ot vo-de-na oh-bee-kol-ka na gra-da. Kak mo-ga da or-ga-nee-zee-ram to-va?*)

931. Do you have any information on overnight buses to the capital?
Имате ли информация за нощни автобуси до столицата?
(*Ee-ma-te li een-for-ma-tsi-ya za nosht-ni av-to-boo-si do sto-lee-tsah-ta?*)

932. I'd like to purchase a travel insurance policy for my trip.
Искам да закупя застраховка за пътуването си.
(*Ee-skam da za-koo-pya zas-trah-hov-ka za put-oo-va-ne-to si.*)

933. Can you recommend a good travel agency for vacation packages?

Можете ли да препоръчате добра туристическа агенция за ваканционни пакети?

(Mo-zhe-te li da pre-poh-ruch-a-te do-bra too-rees-ti-ches-ka ah-gen-tsi-ya za va-kan-tsi-on-ni pa-ke-ti?)

934. I need a seat on the evening ferry to the island.

Трябва ми място на вечерния ферибот за острова.

(Tryab-va mi myas-to na ve-che-rni-ya fe-ri-bot za os-tro-va.)

935. How can I check the departure times for international flights?

Как мога да проверя часовете на тръгване на международни полети?

(Kak mo-ga da pro-ve-rya chas-o-ve-te na trug-va-ne na mezh-doo-narod-ni po-le-ti?)

936. Is there a shuttle service from the hotel to the train station?

Има ли шатъл услуга от хотела до гарата?

(Ee-ma li sha-tul oo-slu-ga ot ho-te-la do ga-ra-ta?)

937. I'd like to charter a private boat for a day trip.

Искам да наема частна лодка за еднодневна екскурзия.

(Ee-skam da na-e-ma chast-na lod-ka za ed-no-dnev-na eks-kur-zi-ya.)

938. Can you assist me in booking a vacation rental apartment?

Можете ли да ми помогнете да резервирам апартамент под наем за ваканцията?

(Mo-zhe-te li da mi po-mog-ne-te da re-zer-vi-ram a-par-ta-ment pod na-em za va-kan-tsi-ya-ta?)

939. I need to arrange transportation for a group of 20 people.
Трябва да организирам транспорт за група от 20 души.
(*Tryab-va da or-ga-ni-zi-ram trans-port za gru-pa ot dvat-tset doo-shi.*)

940. What's the best way to get from the airport to the city center?
Какъв е най-добрият начин да стигна от летището до центъра на града?
(*Ka-kuv e nai-do-bri-yat na-chin da stig-na ot le-ti-she-to do tsehn-tu-ra na gra-da?*)

941. Can you help me find a pet-friendly accommodation option?
Можете ли да ми помогнете да намеря подходящо място за настаняване с домашни любимци?
(*Mo-zhe-te li da mi po-mog-ne-te da na-me-rya pod-ho-dyashto myas-to za na-sta-nyav-a-ne s do-mash-ni lyu-bim-tsi?*)

942. I'd like to plan a road trip itinerary for a scenic drive.
Искам да планирам маршрут за пътешествие с красива панорама.
(*Ee-skam da pla-ni-ram marsh-root za pu-te-she-stvi-e s kra-si-va pa-no-ra-ma.*)

"Старо приятелство не заръжда."
"Old friendship does not rust."
Long-standing friendships are durable and enduring.

Word Search Puzzle: Transport & Directions

CAR
АВТОМОБИЛ
BUS
АВТОБУС
AIRPORT
ЛЕТИЩЕ
SUBWAY
МЕТРО
TAXI
ТАКСИ
STREET
УЛИЦА
MAP
КАРТА
DIRECTION
ПОСОКА
TRAFFIC
ТРАФИК
PARKING
ПАРКИНГ
PEDESTRIAN
ПЕШЕХОДЕЦ
HIGHWAY
МАГИСТРАЛА
BRIDGE
МОСТ
TICKET
БИЛЕТ

```
T  J  O  T  G  C  M  J  M  A  U  A  E  U  T
G  E  W  W  M  C  G  K  P  Q  Y  P  D  P  E
T  N  E  Q  A  T  I  I  K  C  V  A  W  N  Л
C  E  I  R  Л  И  Б  O  M  O  T  B  A  П  И
N  T  K  K  T  B  D  C  H  E  N  J  X  O  Б
B  Q  C  C  R  S  E  O  A  I  F  M  S  C  M
U  D  У  Z  I  A  C  A  V  W  H  E  Q  O  S
J  E  Б  O  N  T  P  T  C  O  M  T  N  K  B
W  X  O  J  N  G  B  W  P  P  P  P  Q  A  R
Л  Е  Т  И  Щ  Е  K  A  P  T  A  O  F  S  T
X  X  B  I  U  X  T  P  B  B  G  H  D  G  Y
U  W  A  Z  M  R  X  R  Z  S  B  U  F  W  B
O  U  R  P  A  B  I  O  A  Z  U  Y  L  E  J
S  L  J  F  H  D  K  W  Ц  G  K  B  J  V  M
V  U  F  E  G  F  L  К  И  Ф  A  P  T  W  A
J  I  B  E  K  K  U  T  Л  W  T  K  Г  S  Г
C  O  K  W  O  G  D  D  У  R  T  N  H  R  И
U  I  B  Z  A  T  F  Z  O  F  A  К  И  T  C
W  A  I  V  A  Y  D  P  H  I  D  K  K  K  T
H  B  D  X  D  L  R  I  R  O  Q  F  P  S  P
Q  X  I  W  J  I  Q  T  R  И  C  K  A  T  A
F  J  E  S  A  L  S  T  H  E  T  S  П  D  Л
W  Z  T  J  V  E  V  Q  U  I  C  B  B  Q  A
E  Q  W  S  D  U  U  F  I  W  G  T  J  C  W
W  L  R  E  Q  A  T  W  K  P  F  H  I  R  Q
I  Q  P  П  Е  Ш  Е  X  O  Д  Е  Ц  W  O  O
V  B  P  P  G  H  M  X  V  Q  V  J  B  A  N
J  A  B  B  W  Q  H  R  D  I  G  G  N  W  Y
M  I  T  J  O  S  H  Z  W  M  O  B  L  I  Y
Q  K  T  B  Z  R  V  I  A  W  U  B  G  Z  Z
```

Correct Answers:

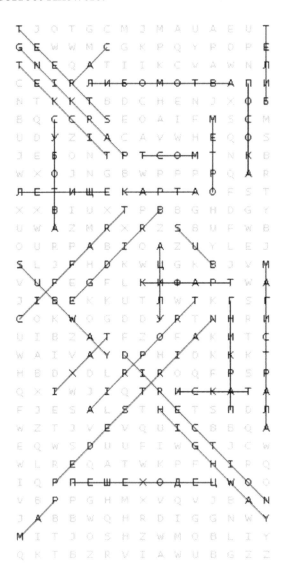

SPECIAL OCCASIONS

- EXPRESSING WELL WISHES AND CONGRATULATIONS -
- CELEBRATIONS AND CULTURAL EVENTS -
- GIVING AND RECEIVING GIFTS -

Expressing Well Wishes & Congratulations

943. Congratulations on your graduation!
Честито завършване!
(*Che-stee-to zah-vur-shvah-ne!*)

944. Best wishes for a long and happy marriage.
Най-добри пожелания за дълъг и щастлив брак.
(*Nai-do-bree po-zhe-la-ni-ya za dul-ug ee shtas-tleev brak.*)

945. Happy anniversary to a wonderful couple.
Честита годишнина на прекрасната двойка.
(*Che-stee-ta go-deesh-nee-na na pre-kras-na-ta dvoi-ka.*)

946. Wishing you a speedy recovery.
Пожелавам ви бързо оздравяване.
(*Po-zhe-la-vam vi bur-zo oz-dra-vya-va-ne.*)

947. Congratulations on your new job!
Честито за новата работа!
(*Che-stee-to za no-va-ta ra-bo-ta!*)

> **Travel Story:** In the Strandzha Mountains, a hiker observed, "Тук природата говори" (Here, nature speaks), appreciating the untouched wilderness.

948. May your retirement be filled with joy and relaxation.
Да бъде пенсионирането ви изпълнено с радост и отдих.
(*Da bu-de pen-si-o-ni-ra-ne-to vi iz-pul-ne-no s ra-dost ee otdih.*)

949. Best wishes on your engagement.
Най-добри пожелания за годежа.
(*Nai-do-bri po-zhe-la-ni-ya za go-de-zha.*)

950. Happy birthday! Have an amazing day.
Честит рожден ден! Имайте страхотен ден.
(*Che-stee-t rozh-den den! Ee-mai-te stra-ho-ten den.*)

> **Cultural Insight:** The Bulgarian Orthodox Church, one
> of the oldest Slavic Orthodox churches, plays a
> significant role in national identity and religious life.

951. Wishing you success in your new venture.
Пожелавам ви успех в новото начинание.
(*Po-zhe-la-vam vi us-peh v no-vo-to na-chi-na-ni-e.*)

952. Congratulations on your promotion!
Честито повишение!
(*Che-stee-to po-vi-she-ni-e!*)

953. Good luck on your exam—you've got this!
Късмет на изпита - ти можеш това!
(*Kus-met na iz-pi-ta - tee mo-zhesh to-va!*)

954. Best wishes for a safe journey.
Пожелавам ви безопасно пътуване.
(*Po-zhe-la-vam vi be-zo-pas-no pu-tu-va-ne.*)

955. Happy retirement! Enjoy your newfound freedom.
Честит пенсиониране! Насладете се на новата си свобода.
(*Che-stee-t pen-si-o-ni-ra-ne! Nas-la-de-te se na no-va-ta si
svo-bo-da.*)

956. Congratulations on your new home.
Честито за новия дом.
(*Che-stee-to za no-vi-ya dom.*)

957. Wishing you a lifetime of love and happiness.
Пожелавам ви цял живот любов и щастие.
(*Po-zhe-la-vam vi tsyal zhi-vot lyu-bov i shtas-tie.*)

958. Best wishes on your upcoming wedding.
Най-добри пожелания за предстоящата сватба.
(*Nai-do-bri po-zhe-la-ni-ya za pred-sto-yash-ta-ta svat-ba.*)

959. Congratulations on the arrival of your baby.
Честито за пристигането на вашето бебе.
(*Che-stee-to za pris-ti-ga-ne-to na va-she-to be-be.*)

960. Sending you warmest thoughts and prayers.
Изпращам ви топли мисли и молитви.
(*Iz-pras-tam vi top-li mis-li i mo-lit-vi.*)

961. Happy holidays and a joyful New Year!
Весели празници и щастлива Нова Година!
(*Ve-se-li praz-ni-tsi i shtas-tli-va No-va Go-di-na!*)

962. Wishing you a wonderful and prosperous future.
Пожелавам ви прекрасно и благоденствено бъдеще.
(*Po-zhe-la-vam vi pre-kras-no i bla-go-den-stve-no bud-esh-te.*)

> **Idiomatic Expression:** "Държа те на думата." -
> Meaning: "I'll hold you to your word."
> (Literal translation: "I hold you to the word.")

Celebrations & Cultural Events

963. I'm excited to attend the festival this weekend.
Радвам се да посетя фестивала този уикенд.
(*Rad-vam se da po-se-tya fes-ti-va-la to-zi ui-kend.*)

964. Let's celebrate this special occasion together.
Нека заедно отпразнуваме този специален повод.
(*Ne-ka zae-dno ot-praz-nu-va-me to-zi spe-tsi-a-len po-vod.*)

> **Fun Fact:** Bulgarian folk tales are a rich tapestry of myths, legends, and historical tales.

965. The cultural parade was a vibrant and colorful experience.
Културният парад беше ярък и цветен преживяване.
(*Kul-tur-ni-yat pa-rad be-she yar-uk i tsve-ten pre-zhi-vya-va-ne.*)

966. I look forward to the annual family reunion.
С нетърпение очаквам годишната семейна среща.
(*S ne-tur-pe-nie o-chak-vam go-dish-na-ta se-mei-na sresh-ta.*)

967. The fireworks display at the carnival was spectacular.
Фойерверките на карнавала бяха зрелищни.
(*Foi-er-ver-ki-te na kar-na-va-la bya-ha zre-lisch-ni.*)

968. It's always a blast at the neighborhood block party.
Винаги е забавно на кварталното блок парти.
(*Vi-na-gi e za-bav-no na kvar-tal-no-to blok par-ti.*)

969.   Attending the local cultural fair is a tradition.
Посещението на местния културен панаир е традиция.
(*Po-se-she-ni-e-to na mes-t-ni-ya kul-tu-ren pa-nair e tra-di-tsi-ya.*)

970.   I'm thrilled to be part of the community celebration.
Радвам се, че съм част от общностното празненство.
(*Rad-vam se, che sam chast ot obsh-nost-no-to praz-nen-stvo.*)

971.   The music and dancing at the wedding were fantastic.
Музиката и танците на сватбата бяха фантастични.
(*Mu-zi-ka-ta i tan-tsi-te na svat-ba-ta bya-ha fan-tas-tich-ni.*)

972.   Let's join the festivities at the holiday parade.
Нека се присъединим към празничните тържества на парада.
(*Ne-ka se pris-ye-di-nim kam praz-nich-ni-te tur-zhes-tva na pa-ra-da.*)

973.   The cultural exchange event was enlightening.
Събитието за културен обмен беше просветляващо.
(*Sa-bi-tie-to za kul-tu-ren ob-men be-she pro-svet-lya-vashto.*)

974.   The food at the international festival was delicious.
Храната на международния фестивал беше вкусна.
(*Hra-na-ta na mezh-du-na-rod-ni-ya fes-ti-val be-she vkus-na.*)

> **Travel Story:** At an icon painting workshop in Etar, the artist shared, "Иконите са прозорци към душата" (Icons are windows to the soul), revealing the spiritual depth of their art.

975.　I had a great time at the costume party.
Чудесно се забавлявах на карнавалното парти.
(Chu-des-no se za-bav-lya-vah na kar-na-val-no-to par-ti.)

976.　Let's toast to a memorable evening!
Наздраве за една запомняща се вечер!
(Naz-dra-ve za ed-na za-pom-nyash-ta se ve-cher!)

977.　The concert was a musical extravaganza.
Концертът беше музикално екстравагантно.
(Kon-tsertat be-she mu-zi-kal-no eks-tra-va-gant-no.)

978.　I'm looking forward to the art exhibition.
Очаквам с нетърпение изложбата на изкуството.
(O-chak-vam s ne-tur-pe-nie iz-lozh-ba-ta na iz-kus-tvo-to.)

979.　The theater performance was outstanding.
Театралното представление беше изключително.
(Te-a-tral-no-to pred-stav-le-nie be-she iz-klyu-chi-tel-no.)

980.　We should participate in the charity fundraiser.
Трябва да участваме в благотворителната кампания.
(Tryab-va da u-chas-tva-me v bla-go-tvo-ri-tel-na-ta kam-pa-ni-ya.)

981.　The sports tournament was thrilling to watch.
Спортният турнир беше вълнуващ за гледане.
(Spor-ti-yat tur-nir be-she vul-nu-vasht za gle-da-ne.)

982.　Let's embrace the local customs and traditions.
Нека приемем местните обичаи и традиции.
(Ne-ka pri-e-mem mes-tni-te o-bi-chai i tra-di-tsi-i.)

Giving and Receiving Gifts

983. I hope you like this gift I got for you.
Надявам се да ти хареса този подарък, който купих за теб.
(*Na-dya-vam se da ti ha-re-sa to-zi po-da-ruk, koy-to ku-pih za teb.*)

984. Thank you for the thoughtful present!
Благодаря за внимателния подарък!
(*Bla-go-da-rya za vni-ma-te-lni-ya po-da-ruk!*)

985. It's a token of my appreciation.
Това е знак на моето признание.
(*To-va e znak na mo-e-to pri-zna-nie.*)

986. Here's a little something to brighten your day.
Ето нещо малко да ти озари деня.
(*E-to neshto mal-ko da ti o-za-ri de-nya.*)

987. I brought you a souvenir from my trip.
Донесох ти сувенир от пътуването си.
(*Do-ne-soh ti su-ve-nir ot pat-u-va-ne-to si.*)

988. This gift is for you on your special day.
Този подарък е за теб за твоя специален ден.
(*To-zi po-da-ruk e za teb za tvo-ya spe-tsi-a-len den.*)

989. I got this with you in mind.
Купих това, като мислех за теб.
(*Ku-pih to-va, ka-to mis-leh za teb.*)

990. You shouldn't have, but I love it!
      Не трябваше, но ми харесва!
      (*Ne tryab-vashe, no mi ha-res-va!*)

991. It's a small gesture of my gratitude.
      Това е малък жест на моята благодарност.
      (*To-va e maluk zhest na mo-ya-ta bla-go-dar-nost.*)

992. I wanted to give you a little surprise.
      Исках да ти поднеса малка изненада.
      (*Is-kah da ti pod-ne-sa mal-ka iz-ne-na-da.*)

993. I hope this gift brings you joy.
      Надявам се този подарък да ти донесе радост.
      (*Na-dya-vam se to-zi po-da-ruk da ti do-ne-se ra-dost.*)

994. It's a symbol of our friendship.
      Това е символ на нашето приятелство.
      (*To-va e sim-bol na na-she-to pri-ya-tel-stvo.*)

995. This is just a token of my love.
      Това е просто знак на моята любов.
      (*To-va e pros-to znak na mo-ya-ta lyu-bov.*)

996. I knew you'd appreciate this.
      Знаех, че ще оцениш това.
      (*Zna-eh, che shte o-tse-nish to-va.*)

997. I wanted to spoil you a bit.
      Исках малко да те разглезя.
      (*Is-kah mal-ko da te raz-gle-zya.*)

998. This gift is for your hard work.
Този подарък е за твоята усърдна работа.
(To-zi po-da-ruk e za tvo-ya-ta oo-sard-na ra-bo-ta.)

999. I hope you find this useful.
Надявам се това да е полезно за теб.
(Na-dya-vam se to-va da e po-lez-no za teb.)

1000. It's a sign of my affection.
Това е знак за моята привързаност.
(To-va e znak za mo-ya-ta pri-var-za-nost.)

1001. I brought you a little memento.
Донесох ти малък спомен.
(Do-ne-soh ti ma-lak spo-men.)

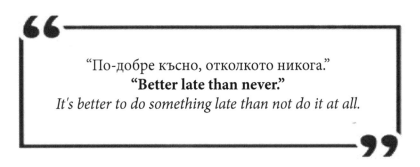

"По-добре късно, отколкото никога."
"Better late than never."
It's better to do something late than not do it at all.

Interactive Challenge: Special Occasions
(Link each English word with their corresponding meaning in Bulgarian)

1) Celebration	Наздравица
2) Gift	Изненада
3) Party	Подарък
4) Anniversary	Сватба
5) Congratulations	Празничен
6) Wedding	Поздравления
7) Birthday	Празненство
8) Graduation	Годишнина
9) Holiday	Рожден ден
10) Ceremony	Празник
11) Tradition	Парти
12) Festive	Церемония
13) Greeting	Поздрав
14) Toast	Традиция
15) Surprise	Завършване

Correct Answers:

1. Celebration - Празненство
2. Gift - Подарък
3. Party - Парти
4. Anniversary - Годишнина
5. Congratulations - Поздравления
6. Wedding - Сватба
7. Birthday - Рожден ден
8. Graduation - Завършване
9. Holiday - Празник
10. Ceremony - Церемония
11. Tradition - Традиция
12. Festive - Празничен
13. Greeting - Поздрав
14. Toast - Наздравица
15. Surprise - Изненада

CONCLUSION

Congratulations on completing "The Ultimate Bulgarian Phrase Book." As you embark on adventures through Bulgaria, from the ancient streets of Plovdiv to the serene beaches of the Black Sea coast, your dedication to mastering Bulgarian is commendable.

This phrasebook has been your steadfast companion, offering a wide array of phrases and expressions to enhance your communication and enrich your experience. You've navigated through basic greetings like "Здравей" (Zdravei) and "Добър ден" (Dobar den) to more complex phrases, equipping yourself for a range of interactions and a deeper appreciation of Bulgaria's rich cultural tapestry.

Embarking on a language learning journey is an enriching endeavor. Your efforts have established a solid foundation in Bulgarian. Remember, language is more than a communication tool; it's a bridge to understanding a culture's soul and essence.

If this phrasebook has been a part of your language learning adventure, I'd love to hear your story! Feel free to reach out on Instagram: **@adriangruszka**. Share your experiences, ask for advice, or simply say "Здравей!" If you mention this book on social media and tag me, I'd be thrilled to celebrate your progress in Bulgarian.

For further resources, detailed insights, and updates, visit **www.adriangee.com**. There, you'll find additional materials, including recommended courses and a community of language enthusiasts ready to support your continuing journey.

Learning Bulgarian opens doors to new connections and viewpoints. Your passion for learning and adapting is your greatest asset in this linguistic venture. Embrace every chance to learn, engage, and deepen your understanding of Bulgarian culture and life.

Успех (Uspeh - Good luck)! Keep practicing diligently, honing your skills, and most importantly, enjoying every moment of your Bulgarian language journey.

Благодаря (Blagodarya - Thank you) for choosing this phrasebook. May your future travels be rich with meaningful conversations and insights as you delve deeper into the fascinating world of languages!

- Adrian Gee